A2 in a Week

Sociology

Michael Orr-Love,
Abbey College, Birmingham
Series Editor: Kevin Byrne

Where to find the information you need

SUCCESS OR YOUR MONEY BACK

Letts' market leading series A2 in a Week gives you everything you need for exam success. We're so confident that they're the best revision books you can buy that if you don't make the grade we will give you your money back!

HERE'S HOW IT WORKS

Register the Letts A2 in a Week guide you buy by writing to us within 28 days of purchase with the following information:

- Name
- Address
- Postcode
- Subject of A2 in a Week book bought

Please include your till receipt

To make a **claim**, compare your results to the grades below. If any of your grades qualify for a refund, make a claim by writing to us within 28 days of getting your results, enclosing a copy of your original exam slip. If you do not register, you won't be able to make a claim after you receive your results.

CLAIM IF...

You are an A2 (A Level) student and do not get grade E or above. You are a Scottish Higher level student and do not get a grade C or above.
This offer is not open to Scottish students taking SCE Higher Grade, or Intermediate qualifications.

Letts Educational
Chiswick Centre
414 Chiswick High Road
London W4 5TF

Tel: 020 8996 3333
Fax: 020 8742 8390
e-mail: mail@lettsed.co.uk
website: www.letts-education.com

Registration and claim address:
Letts Success or Your Money Back Offer, Letts Educational, Chiswick Centre, 414 Chiswick High Road, London W4 5TF

TERMS AND CONDITIONS

1. Applies to the Letts A2 in a Week series only
2. Registration of purchases must be received by Letts Educational within 28 days of the purchase date
3. Registration must be accompanied by a valid till receipt
4. All money back claims must be received by Letts Educational within 28 days of receiving exam results
5. All claims must be accompanied by a letter stating the claim and a copy of the relevant exam results slip
6. Claims will be invalid if they do not match with the original registered subjects
7. Letts Educational reserves the right to seek confirmation of the level of entry of the claimant
8. Responsibility cannot be accepted for lost, delayed or damaged applications, or applications received outside of the stated registration/claim timescales
9. Proof of posting will not be accepted as proof of delivery
10. Offer only available to A2 students studying within the UK
11. SUCCESS OR YOUR MONEY BACK is promoted by Letts Educational, Chiswick Centre, 414 Chiswick High Road, London W4 5TF
12. Registration indicates a complete acceptance of these rules
13. Illegible entries will be disqualified
14. In all matters, the decision of Letts Educational will be final and no correspondence will be entered into

Every effort has been made to trace copyright holders and obtain their permission for the use of copyright material. The authors and publishers will gladly receive information enabling them to rectify any error or omission in subsequent editions.

First published 2001
Reprinted 2002

Text © Michael Orr-Love 2001
Design and illustration © Letts Educational Ltd 2001

PORTSMOUTH
CENTRAL LIBRARY
TEL: 023 9281 9311

All our Rights Reserved. No part of this publication may be reproduced, stored in a retrieval system, or transmitted, in any form or by any means, electronic, mechanical, photocopying, recording or otherwise, without the prior permission of Letts Educational.

British Library Cataloguing in Publication Data
A CIP record for this book is available from the British Library.

ISBN 1 85805 921 6

Prepared by *specialist* publishing services, Milton Keynes

Printed in Italy

PORTSMOUTH CITY COUNCIL LIBRARY SERVICE

301.

C800081766

Letts Educational Limited is a division of Granada Learning Limited, part of the Granada Media Group

Stratification – Inequality and Difference

20 minutes

Test your knowledge

1 Since 1971, the _____ _____ scheme has been used to measure official statistics. The Registrar-General was replaced by _____ _____ _____ . _____ scheme of classification has been used by academics conducting mobility studies. Stanworth argues that by excluding _____ it gives an incomplete account.

2 The idea that anyone can succeed is known as _____. Glass, Blau and Duncan (1949) found that _____ _____ mobility is rare.

3 _____ _____ refers to the chances of individuals moving up or down the social ladder. _____ _____ occurs when there are movement and changes in the size of each class.

4 Saunders disputes the existence of an all-embracing, all-powerful 'ruling class' but locates instead '_____ _____ _____ _____'. Dahrendorf describes this as _____ _____ . Scott describes the upper class as having a _____ _____ _____ . In particular, the Marxist, Ralph _____ and Giddens identify a distinct, unified capitalist upper class.

5 Typically, the middle class has three distinct sections: the _____ middle class (owners of small businesses), the 'new' middle class, which is comprised of an _____ and lower strata. The former is described by Goldthorpe as a '_____' class. Lower middle-class occupations tend to include occupations such as _____ and _____. Braverman argued that the middle class has become more '_____' because of de-skilling.

6 The working class can be divided into what Lockwood describes as the _____ and Crewe's _____ working class. The former would be recognised for its strong sense of working-class solidarity, whereas the latter is seen as having undergone _____.

7 The _____ is seen as a distinct group of people who form a layer beneath the working class. Some theorists, such as Murray, believe that their lowly position can be attributed to their being _____ _____.

8 The functionalist account describes the _____ of differentiation. The Marxist account describes class _____ between two distinct groups: the proletariat and the bourgeoisie. The _____ account bases class on three levels: economic, status and power.

Answers

1 General Register, Standard Occupational Classification, Goldthorpe's, women **2** meritocracy, long range **3** Relative mobility, Absolute mobility **4** an influential economic elite, class decomposition, constellation of interests, Miliband **5** traditional, upper, service, nurses, teachers, proletarianised **6** traditional, new, embourgeoisement **7** underclass, welfare dependent **8** inevitability, conflict, Weberian

 If you got them all right, skip to page 14

3

Stratification – Inequality and Difference

40 minutes

Improve your knowledge

Social stratification refers to the structured inequalities and division of society into strata, like geological layers, with the most favoured groups occupying the top layers and the best life-chances (culturally and financially). In the next three chapters we will consider the competing accounts. Some see social status as a determinant of life chances, and argue that the overlapping, interdependent (but never mutually exclusive) 'identities' of class, ethnicity, sex and age impact on everyday living. Post-modern or post-structural theories, however, emphasise the fluidity and changeable nature of 'purchasable' identities.

1 Measuring social class

The classification of social class by public institutions and academics alike (for the purpose of mobility studies) has proven to be an elusive task. This section will look at:

- official measurements of social class

- alternative categories.

Since 1971, the Registrar-General Scheme has divided class into six categories. A distinction is made between manual (IIIM, IV and V) and non-manual occupations (I, II and IIINM), which assumes that categories reflect how society regards each occupation. It is not based on earning potential but status classification. It has been the main way in which class is measured in official statistics. The Registrar-General was replaced by National Statistics Socio-economic Classification (NS-SEC), which classifies jobs according to their skill level and the qualifications needed to occupy them.

Goldthorpe's scheme of classification has been used by academics conducting mobility studies. It is made up of several factors: market situation (how much you earn, etc.) and work situation (control and autonomy over work). He devised the following classes: service class I made up of higher grade professionals and large proprietors, and service class II made up of lower grade professionals, for example, administrators and higher grade technicians. The intermediate group III are comprised of routine non-manual, largely clerical

4

workers. Small proprietors make up group IV, and lower grade technicians fall into group V. The working class is divided into skilled manual workers (group VI) and semi- and unskilled workers (group VII).

A major criticism of these classificatory systems is that they are male-centric – women's class position is dictated by their husband's. According to Stanworth, by excluding women it gives an incomplete account. Feminist classificatory schemes discard the concept of the head of household. The Surrey University scheme divides men and women, part-time, full-time and unwaged employment and shows the different occupational structure for men and women. It is thought also to highlight the different living patterns experienced in cross-class relationships.

Runciman (1990) devised an alternative scheme based on the aggregate of roles of different individuals. Each class position has people with very different roles that can be categorised as similar. This is based on what Runciman describes as three types of power: ownership, control and marketability. Individuals may possess different amounts of each, which determines class position. Those at the bottom of the social ladder tend to have little or no control over production, have very little wealth and few marketable skills. The upper class has disproportionately more wealth, power and control than others.

2 Social mobility

For any liberal, democratic country to be based on meritocracy, it must have social mobility. People should be able to compete for occupational positions equally, but this does not ensure equality of outcome. However, the idea that *anyone* can succeed is a misconception, because there are only a few positions at the top of the occupational ladder.

We will be concerned with the following:

- arguments that claim mobility has increased since 1944

- arguments that claim mobility is static.

Glass, Blau and Duncan (1949) found in their studies that long-range mobility is rare. Mobility is either vertical (up or down) or horizontal (for example, moving into another region). Downward mobility is less common than upward mobility.

People tend to move downwards when they are made redundant. Women experience this downward mobility especially when they are divorced or separated. Intra-generational studies are concerned with how individuals move up or down in the course of their lifetime. Intergenerational mobility measures whether children enter the same type of occupations as their parents and grandparents. More often than not, people follow in their parents' footsteps.

Relative mobility refers to the chances of individuals moving up or down the social ladder. Lipset, Bendix and Payne found considerable upward movement from blue-collar to white-collar work. The Nuffield study also found that the proportion of people in the top two classes had increased. The service class *had* increased and it needed to recruit from outside of the middle class, hence upward mobility. Absolute mobility occurs when there are movement and changes in the size of each class and for many sociologists this indicates that upward mobility is a misnomer. According to Goldthorpe and Lockwood, social movement can be attributed to changing occupational structure rather than to society becoming more meritocratic. The shrinkage of working-class jobs and expansion of the middle class has protected the middle class from downward mobility.

In addition, it appears that the social reforms of 1944 have done nothing to change the social structure. The prime beneficiaries were the middle class; studies by Halsey, Heath and Ridge showed that children born into the service class were several times more likely to stay in their class position than working-class children achieving service status. In addition, middle-class families enjoy material and cultural advantages over their working-class counterparts, whose lack of cultural capital acts as a barrier to upward mobility. The right wing theorist Saunders believes that social inequality is based on IQ and that the superior upbringing of middle-class children ensures their class situation.

3 The upper class

Unquestionably, an upper class exists. In terms of numbers it is very small but it would appear to be disproportionately powerful, culturally, politically and economically. For example, the most wealthy 10% own 50% of the wealth, the top 20% of households receive 50% of total income, whilst the top 1% in the UK own 75% of shares. In reviewing ideas on the upper class, we will concentrate on accounts that suggest:

- the balance of power and structure of the upper class has changed

- the upper class still constitutes a single, coherent group that dominates society to serve its own interests.

Central to the debate is the question of who actually make up this social elite and to what extent do they 'rule' society? Writers such as Saunders dispute the existence of an all-embracing, all-powerful 'ruling class' but locate instead an 'influential economic elite' consisting of high-powered, highly paid managers. They may own a percentage of the company they work for but do not by any means constitute a 'capitalist class' of their own – for example, they do not control the agencies of the state. Dahrendorf argues similarly that upper class decomposition has taken place through the prevalence of share ownership and the control and day-to-day running of business by managers rather than owners. This has resulted in a dilution of power because the upper class can no longer selfishly pursue its own interests. For example, owners can be drawn into conflict with managers, whose interests may not be wholly compatible with or serviceable to owners; they are also answerable to shareholders, unions and governments.

Giddens and Westergaard and Resler reject Dahrendorf's (re: Burnham's) 'managerial revolution', stating that managers and owners are similar enough to be considered as a single, coherent upper strata; they share a common interest of success and profitability. This is what Scott describes as a 'constellation of interests' held by people who own their own (big) businesses, those who act as representatives for banks (finance) and high-paid, high-powered managers. Although the shape of the upper class has changed, Scott, Miliband and Giddens identify a capitalist upper class, which is a distinct, unified group of people with similar and interconnected patterns of wealth (not dependent on income), cultural capital and privileged educational and life chances (e.g. attending public schools and Oxford or Cambridge universities).

4 The middle class

The middle class can be distinguished from the upper class in terms of its relative lack of wealth and prestige, and from the working class by virtue of its being made up of those with non-manual occupations; they are neither bourgeois nor proletariat. Competing accounts focus on:

- the growth of the middle class

- the 'proletarianisation' of the middle class.

In its general usage, the term 'middle class' embraces a vast array of occupations and concomitant market situations. It is held that middle-class people enjoy higher status, better life chances, healthier and safer working conditions and better pay and benefits than manual workers.

Former prime minister John Major's declaration of a 'classless society' reflects an optimistic, common-sense notion that the middle class has grown to such an extent (due to rise in incomes, home and share ownership) that we can all now be considered as middle class. It would appear from this standpoint that only those people who occupy the minority groups at each end of society constitute a distinct group. Typically, the middle class has three distinct sections, made up of the 'old' middle class (self-employed, owners of small businesses) and the 'new' middle class, which is comprised of an upper and lower strata. The upper middle class is described by Goldthorpe as the 'service' class because they possess the specialised (and highly marketable) knowledge and managerial know-how to service the needs of employers. Mills describes a 'power elite', arguing that the barriers to entry (specialised qualifications allowing membership of professional bodies) to professions such as law and high-level management create a privileged market position which affords them greater status, income and material possessions than other middle-class occupations.

Lower middle-class occupations tend to include those employed as sales representatives, teachers, nurses and so on. However, there are still varying 'market situations' between different occupations and the debate centres on how and where to delineate between middle-class and working-class statuses. Braverman, looking at the issue from a Marxist perspective, argues that companies have inevitably become larger (by monopolising markets). Work has become more specialised and fragmented (a clerical production line), and this has led to the 'proletarianisation' of middle-class professional occupations; in other words, they require less skill. Less skill reflects a decline in occupational category and market situation and the creation of a working-class consciousness. Many people in lower middle-class occupations find themselves in a 'contradictory class' location because they perform non-manual work but have a lower income than those workers employed in manual (thus lower status) occupations. Goldthorpe recognises this conundrum but still insists that clerical and many other non-manual occupations maintain a better market situation than manual workers by enjoying, on average, better working conditions, longer holidays, better fringe benefits and greater autonomy. Goldthorpe proposes that this group of workers constitutes a new intermediate class, neither working class nor middle class.

5 The working class

This section will review the distinctions between:

- the different tiers of the working class

- traditional versus new working class, concentrating on the 'embourgeoisement' thesis.

Like the other classes, the working class can be divided into tiers: the upper tier ('central', skilled workers who enjoy well-paid, stable work) and the lower tier ('peripheral', unskilled and semi-skilled workers). Furthermore, it can be argued that divisions between tiers are exacerbated by unions, who represent the interests of their members by employing forms of social closure. It is generally agreed that the market situation and life chances of those occupying working-class positions are worse than those of the middle class. The working class experience poorer health, shorter life-expectancy, poorer living and working conditions, educational under-achievement, and an increased likelihood of being unemployed, a convicted criminal or a victim of crime. Many writers have used class to focus on class self-image and group identity, locating different sub-cultural activities and practices (re: Bourdieu's habitus). Lockwood's 'traditional proletariat' appears on the surface to contrast significantly with Crewe's 'new' working class. The former would be recognised for their strong sense of working-class solidarity and sociability (centred on working men's clubs), collectivism, living and working in close-knit communities, and often being reliant on 'traditional' industry (e.g. mining, shipbuilding, steel works). In contrast, the new working class are southern based, comparatively well-paid, employed by private industry, are home owners and enjoy different patterns of sociability (more privatised). However, to suggest that these workers are not working class would be considered by Goldthorpe et al as premature – they refute the 'embourgeoisement' thesis. Despite the absence of a 'them and us' mentality, union membership remains strong, even if the goals are somewhat self-orientated. Workers still have a wholly instrumental attitude to work and do not display middle-class attitudes to career and patterns of socialising. Finally, Britain has undergone deindustrialisation: manufacturing has declined and two million traditional proletarian jobs were lost between 1979 and 1994. These were replaced by mainly service industry jobs but these bear all the hallmarks of limited skill, production-line work which render them categorically as occupations belonging to the working class.

6 The underclass

The underclass is seen as a distinct group of people who form a layer beneath the working class. For a long time, sociologically and politically, theorists have shared a preoccupation with behaviour that contradicts the norms and values of society. This review will cover:

- who and what constitutes the underclass

- individualistic versus structural theories.

Typically, the underclass is described as having a combination of some (but not necessarily all) of the following economic and 'cultural' characteristics:

- multiply deprived (economically and culturally)

- single-parent families

- poor living conditions

- belong to an ethnic minority group

- unemployed

- criminal/violent

- marginalised from 'mainstream' society.

It should be borne in mind that history has shown that the categorisation and subsequent treatment of 'deviants' (re: Foucault's discourses) has often taken on a more insidious form. Political regimes such as Nazi Germany have dispensed with their 'underclass' through a systematic programme of genocide.

Some right-wing critics suggest that deviant behaviour is genetic. For example, Murray, echoing the work of Hayek (*Road to Serfdom*) has argued that the short-term, dependent culture of black Americans is inherited socially through the increase of provisions by the welfare ('nanny') state. Because of welfare-dependence, a culture of poverty ensues and there is little reason for people to build solid communities because self-sufficiency is discouraged. Murray also detected an underclass in Britain, but this is not a reference to the degree but to the type of poverty. He argues that this group's position is entirely of their own making – they are ill-schooled, badly behaved, unkempt, prone to drug and alcohol addiction, dishonest and work-shy. Dahrendorf treats the existence of an underclass more sympathetically – as a cancer created by changes in the patterns of work (the need for fewer workers and low wages) which inevitably trap people, even if they 'play the game'. Is it any wonder, when there is little chance of escaping poverty, that people decide to opt out of mainstream society?

Marx stressed the importance and intrinsic satisfaction of individuals engaging in productive and creative work. However, he located a group who have their own world view, the lumpenproletariat, who by opting out of the economic system become a 'dangerous class', not just because they typically indulge in undesirable/destructive types of behaviour but also because they act as a reserve army of labour (whose labour is likely to be cheaper). Other workers are less likely to form a radical class consciousness if they feel undermined by the existence of such people and their potential ability to replace them (described by Giddens as a secondary labour market).

 ## 7 Different theories and explanations of stratification

This section will look at the following competing theories:

- the functionalist account, which describes the inevitability of differentiation

- The Marxist account that sees class as two distinct, competing groups

- The Weberian account, which bases class on three levels: economic, status and power.

The functionalist account, as espoused by Durkheim, Parsons, Davis and Moore and Spencer, stresses the 'functional necessity' of stratification in modern societies, which are highly specialised and interdependent. Inevitably, according to Davis and Moore, stratification takes place in all societies and the social order is an expression of societies' core values. For example, a capitalist society rewards the most productive or important people. Their analysis assumes that people are not born equal; some are 'naturally' more functional to society than others. However, Tumin (echoing Durkheim) criticises this account for overlooking 'social closure' (Giddens) or the 'barriers of entry' (for example, racism) that prevent a true meritocracy from existing. On this basis alone, stratification has proven to be divisive rather than promoting social stability.

According to Marxist analysis, class is an objective fact of capitalism. Production is a centrally defining human activity and the ownership or otherwise of the means of production is the expression of the class system ultimately based upon, and a product of, exploitation (surplus value). The interests of the two classes are diametrically opposed; to survive, the working class must sell their labour to the bourgeoisie who own the means of production and protect their interests forcefully and ideologically. As with all historical moments (re: 'dialectical materialism'), Marx predicted a clash, expressed in a polarised and collective 'class consciousness', of the working class against the ruling class, as the gap between rich and poor grew wider. This conflict would inevitably result in a new and final era of history, when communism replaced capitalism.

Neo-Marxists use Marx's typology as the basis of investigation, even though the concept of class in today's world appears to be more complex than Marx originally envisaged. This complexity can be explained away quite simply, even though many people (especially the affluent working class and middle class) do not experience the 'proletariat' condition (poverty). Wright argues that many people occupy a 'contradictory class position'. In between the working and ruling classes are groups of people who are 'contradictory' because they are neither capitalists nor manual workers. Wright identifies three dimensions to stratification: well-paid, well-placed individuals may exercise control over investments/money capital, the physical means of production and labour power, but they do not and cannot control them all, only capitalists control each one of these dimensions. Theirs is a double bind – they are both the exploiters and the exploited. Accompanying this is Braverman's assertion that two-thirds of the population should be categorised as 'working class' despite the apparent decrease in working-class and concomitant increase in middle-class occupations.

Fundamentally, people still have to sell their labour and are thus working class, by virtue of the fact that they are 'hired' (this idea was also espoused by former Labour leader Neil Kinnock in the 1992 general election campaign). Braverman clearly believes, as did Marx, that the 'proletarianisation' of the workplace will make the polarity between the proletariat and the ruling class more stark. Occupations, especially those formerly reserved for the middle class (see Weber's typology later) are undergoing a process of de-skilling. The proletarian class consciousness will surface as a consequence (the realisation that despite perceived differences, workers belong to the same exploited class) and a change in social relations will become inevitable.

8 Although there is a degree of convergence between Weber's and Marx's work, Weber contested that class is simply a reflection of the ownership or non-ownership of the means of production. Weber *did* argue that ownership of wealth/property is the basis of the class system, but he also argued that stratification has other dimensions. Weber was also interested in the relationship between class, which is derived from economic means, status (social position) and party (political allegiance). In contemporary society, a person's class situation is also their market situation; it is a measure of their life chances and the skills and services they have to offer the economy. Weber argued that even though class and status are often inextricably linked, it is status rather than class that forms the basis of commonality and collective action, which weakens the possibility of working-class solidarity (what Dahrendorf labelled as decomposition) that Marx envisaged. Status is often derived from economic means but it is also expressed through occupation (different occupations are accorded different statuses) and adopting particular lifestyles (conspicuous consumption). Weber also argued that political power could be separated from economic power, and that membership of political groups (party) does not necessarily reflect class lines, so people from very disparate groups share the same interests, aims and objectives (e.g. working-class and middle-class Conservatives). Weber devised four broad categories of class: upper class, petit bourgeoisie, middle class and working class – but argued that instead of a sharp division between each, the situation was blurred by people's membership of status and party 'communities'.

45 minutes

Use your knowledge

1 Does the growth of the middle class imply greater social movement?

2 'Class can only be based on income.' Discuss.

3 Discuss the view that the upper class is a cohesive social group.

Stratification – Sex and Gender

20 minutes

Test your knowledge

1 Non-sociological accounts of gender argue that differences between men and women are _____. Functionalists argue that society reflects the natural order. Murdock stresses the 'logical' division of labour, because _____ are stronger than _____ and more suited to physical labour.

2 Most sociologists work from the premise that gender roles are _____ rather than _____ determined.

3 Feminist sociology is primarily concerned with _____. Engels argued that the emergence of _____ _____ created the conditions of female oppression. _____ _____ such as Firestone argue that men have a natural physical superiority because they do not _____ _____. Marxist feminism, espoused by Rowbotham et al, focuses on the double bind of patriarchy and _____. _____ _____ have been particularly virulent in their critique of 'mainstream' feminism, arguing that ethnicity is overlooked. Walby offers a _____ _____ _____ , which recognises the different but interconnected 'systems of patriarchy'.

4 Many inequalities still exist in relation to gender and paid employment. Historically, women have been employed in _____ _____ jobs. Men tend to dominate the higher professions and most areas of management. The _____ _____ Act has narrowed the gap between male and female earners but there are still discrepancies at all levels. Braverman describes women as a _____ _____ _____ _____. The functionalist account prefers to explain women's secondary position in terms of _____ _____ theory. Women are more likely to have career breaks for motherhood and so there is less incentive to invest in them.

5 The first wave feminists campaigned for legal and political rights at the start of the 20th century. An example of these were the _____. The second wave of activity, which has promoted the female perspective, is known as the _____ _____ _____.

Answers

1 natural, men, women **2** socially, biologically **3** patriarchy, private property, Radical feminists, give birth, capitalism, Black feminists, triple systems theory **4** lower status, Equal Opportunities, reserve army of labour, human capital **5** Suffragettes, Women's Liberation Movement

 If you got them all right, skip to page 21

30 minutes

Improve your knowledge

1 Non-sociological and functionalist accounts of gender

Non-sociological or biological accounts argue that:

- the differences between men and women are natural

- society reflects natural order.

Because of the apparent universality of social roles, everyday discourses on male and female traits position them as natural and 'God-given'. In particular, Sociobiologists rely upon either evolutionary accounts or argue that behaviour is governed by genetic structures (brain lateralisation, physicality and hormones) to explain why men and women occupy different roles in society. It is argued that males and females produce different levels of testosterone (which is linked with aggression), androgens, progesterone and oestrogen. These are linked with the activity of the nervous system and so can influence behaviour, personality and emotional disposition.

Barash and Wilson explain men's dominance and possessiveness over women by arguing that whereas women can be certain whether a child is her own, a man cannot and will want to control the woman's sexual activity to ensure his genes are passed on rather than another man's. Although these claims are hotly disputed, theorists such as Tiger and Fox argue that biology lags behind the huge advancements in culture, hence the lack of fit between 'natural' roles and 'new' ideas regarding the roles of men and women.

Similarly, the functionalist account, as espoused by Murdock, stresses that the biological differences between men and women lead to a 'logical' division of labour – for instance, men are stronger than women and more suited to physical labour, whereas women are also more likely to be tied to, or around the home because of childbirth. Parsons describes the woman's role as expressive, naturally predisposed to provide warmth, security and emotional support to the family unit.

2 Conflict approaches

This section will: query the perceived naturalness of sex/gender roles; argue that gender roles are socially constructed.

Key points from AS in a Week
Socialisation (nature versus nurture) pages 14–15
The family (feminist accounts) pages 29–30
Health and gender page 54
Work (post-Fordism) pages 59–60
Unemployment pages 62–63
Education and gender pages 74–75

Inevitably, the biological accounts have been contested on many fronts. For example, scientists have conducted animal experiments which show that rats injected with testosterone are more aggressive and more likely to fight. However, there are inherent problems in applying animal behaviour to humans. Experiments often ignore the influence of environmental factors on behaviour. Bleier points out that this argument does not explain male dominance in spheres other than fighting. Other accounts are ethnocentric, wrongly stressing the 'naturalness' and applicability to white, capitalist society.

Marx argued that all inequalities are not natural but based on historical conditions. In other words, the dominance of men over women is ideological – it is culturally constructed and maintained. Most sociologists work from the premise that gender roles are socially rather than biologically determined. Oakley, echoing the work of de Beauvoir, argues that there is no correlation between sex and gender; one is not born but rather becomes a woman. The link between childbirth and the caring and nurturing role appears to be one of the more persuasive and natural reasons for women to stay at home, but Oakley showed that this could be handed over to someone else and not detrimentally affect the child's development in any way.

 ## Feminism

Feminist sociology is primarily concerned with patriarchy describing and accounting for the unequal distribution of wealth and opportunity between men and women.

The differing and competing feminist accounts

According to feminist accounts, the issue of sex and gender is one of the most profound examples of a stratification system. Men have more wealth, status and influence than women. Women are described as being subordinate, oppressed and exploited. Engels accepted that, historically, roles were segregated, not as a product of male dominance but of mutual interdependence and allocation. The emergence of private property was accompanied by primogeniture (first-born male inheriting property) and males wishing to hold on to their wealth (livestock) were required to restrict female sexual choices so that they were certain of parentage.

The radical feminist Firestone argued that patriarchy has manifested itself through the different physical characteristics of males and females. Men have a natural physical superiority because they do not have childbearing roles. Ultimately, this is what confines women's experiences and Firestone argues that this can only be resolved by advancing reproductive technology (so children grow outside of the body) and women can be freed from their 'duties' as mother, carer and homemaker.

Marxist feminism, espoused by Rowbotham *et al*, focuses on the double bind of patriarchy and capitalism. In particular, Marxist feminists focus on the home as the site of the physical and ideological reproduction of 'good' workers for the capitalist system. The unequal relationships inherent in capitalism – exploitation, subservience, little or no rewards (intrinsic and extrinsic) – are acted out within the home.

Black feminists have been particularly virulent in their critique of 'mainstream' feminism, arguing that the experience of ethnicity has been overlooked and that 'mainstream' feminism is ethnocentrically white (and middle class). In the worldview of white feminists, patriarchy and racism may be seen as distinct, but they act together in the oppression and everyday experience of black women. Walby's triple systems theory is an account of patriarchal power which recognises that 'systems of patriarchy' are intersected by class, 'race' and gender. The 'patriarchal structures' can be identified in the public and private sphere, for example in the modes of production, through exploitation in both the workplace and the home, through state policies that operate in the interests of men, through male violence towards women, through sexual harassment and rape in the public sphere and in the home.

 ## Gender and work

Despite the number of legislative and attitudinal advances towards women, there are still inequalities in gender and paid employment. We will concentrate on:

- women experiencing poorer working conditions

- the competing accounts that explain women's secondary position.

In work, women tend to be the most expendable. Men and women are not equally represented in the occupational structure. Historically, women have been employed in lower status jobs; two-thirds do routine non-manual and manual work. Men also tend to dominate industries such as construction and engineering, whereas women are more likely to be employed in education and health. Men tend to dominate the higher professions and most areas of management. The Equal Pay Act (1970) and the Sex Discrimination Act (1975) narrowed the gap between male and female earners but there are still discrepancies at all levels.

Since the early 1960s, as a result of the changing economy, the proportion of women employed has increased significantly and women now make up over 40% of the workforce. Braverman describes women as a reserve army of labour, arguing that changes in work practices have de-skilled jobs, and they have been recruited as a suitable source because many employers prefer unskilled workers. Similarly, McDowell's analysis found that 'new' job opportunities created by post-Fordist working practices tend to favour women. These 'new' jobs, found mainly in the service sector, are closer to traditional female occupations. However, 'new' work conditions are also comparable on many fronts; women are peripheral workers – their work is characterised by short-term contracts, no statutory rights to sick pay or holiday pay and no representation.

Walby insists that unions are problematic, because they are patriarchal institutions, dominated by men and working for men's interests. With the introduction of new technology and more women entering the workplace, unions have 'protected' their members by isolating the female workforce, fearing that acceptance will result in downgrading, lower pay and benefits. As a consequence, women are less politically powerful and less organised/unionised than men. Stanko argues that sexual harassment at work prevents women from being taken seriously in the workplace and results in the down-grading of many women's jobs.

The functionalist account uses human capital theory to explain, in general, why women occupy lower status jobs. Women are more likely to have career breaks for motherhood and so there is less incentive to invest in them. They also lag behind male employees by missing out on training opportunities and gaining qualifications and experience. Furthermore, women also suffer the double burden of bringing up children as well as working. Despite this, Martin and Roberts argue that it is now expected that both spouses work, and as more women work, more *want* to work. Women who do not opt for family life tend to follow similar career paths to men.

Feminist political activity

Historically, women have been seen as inferior to men, mostly because they have been deprived of educational and cultural opportunities. This section is primarily concerned with explaining:

- how women have challenged preconceptions through political action

- how ideas and values regarding gender roles have changed.

Feminist activity has taken two forms. The first wave feminists campaigned for legal and political rights at the start of the 20th Century. Suffragettes were involved with direct action, actively seeking to gain voting rights for women and improving working conditions and safety standards. The second wave of activity has promoted the female perspective, concerned primarily with civil rights issues, women's control over their bodies and equality in the work place. For example, the Women's Liberation Movement raised women's consciousness and awareness of problems specific to women. Contraception has become widely available and to an extent has undermined patriarchy. Women no longer have to commit themselves to a lifetime of parental toil. However, the question remains: can true equality for women ever be achieved? What approach should women take? Should women see themselves as essentially the same as men? Or can their interests be realised by expressing these differences? Butler argues that women conspire against themselves by asking the wrong questions and assuming the wrong answers. According to Gilligan, women do not have to become men because they have different and precious moral concerns. Women have an ethic of care, which has developed through nurturing and caring for children.

Recent work by Wilkinson and Mulgan has highlighted age as being a significant attitudinal factor towards sex/gender roles. There is evidence of a major difference between the values of the old and the young. The 1990s have witnessed a convergence of male and female ideas and values. Young males engage in traditional 'feminine' tasks, whilst women are taking a more 'masculine' outlook (re: the 'ladette'). Younger women are spending less time engaged in household work and more likely to participate in the public sphere.

Stratification – Sex and Gender

45 minutes

Use your knowledge

1. 'Women's roles are natural and inevitable.' Discuss.

2. Are women still second-class citizens?

Stratification – Ethnicity and Race

25 minutes

Test your knowledge

1 The term 'race' has many negative connotations, so sociologists tend to favour the term _____ to describe people's differences. This broader term emphasises cultural rather than perceived _____ differences. Foucault argued that once you begin to classify you start to _____. This was true in the work of earlier sociobiologists, such as Samuel James Morton, who developed a _____ of 'races'. Steve Jones argues that the colour of somebody's skin does not say much about what is under it. _____ differences cannot be attributed to physical ones.

2 Racism can be defined as _____ and holding preconceived ideas about groups of people. Essentially, racism is a _____ of _____ about the apparent differences between 'races'. _____ is the 'theory' put into practice; it is the unequal treatment of various racial groups. The term _____ _____ refers to the set of in-built exclusionary practices in an organisation.

3 The Frankfurt School devised the theory of the _____ _____. Adorno et al argued that early socialisation without warmth and love leads to racist tendencies in individuals. Cashmore describes racism as a type of natural _____ which surfaces when people defend the established order of things. The BCCCS identified a _____ _____. Instead of racism based on perceived 'natural' differences, it was based on _____ differences.

4 The 1948 _____ _____ _____ allowed all citizens of the Commonwealth to enter the UK to work and settle. However, since then most laws have concentrated on limiting immigration. Immigration by _____ people has been defined as a 'problem'. For example, in 1988, would-be immigrants had to pass a '_____ _____ _____ _____ _____'. Castles and Miller argue that _____ has created the need to migrate. The functionalist account argues that conflict is derived from cultural differences, which undermine the _____ _____.

5 Ethnicity is another _____ system. In the labour market, there are straightforward links between _____ and prejudice and the predominance of ethnic minorities occupying lower paid work. Brown and Gay's _____ _____ project showed that white applicants were received more positively than black applicants.

Answers

1 ethnicity, biological, judge, hierarchy, Behavioural 2 prejudiced way thinking, Racialism, institutional racism 3 authoritarian personality, conservatism, new racism, cultural 4 British Nationality Act, black, independent of public funds test, colonialism, social consensus 5 stratification, discrimination, application test

✔ If you got them all right, skip to page 29

Stratification – Ethnicity and Race

30 minutes

Improve your knowledge

Key points from AS in a Week

Ethnicity   page 16

Post-modern identities
            pages 20–21

Unemployment
            page 62

Education (labelling and achievement)
            pages 71–75

1 Biological and cultural explanations of 'race' and ethnicity

The term 'human race' (race as lineage) implies that all humans come from the same point of origin and that they are all the same and equal. However, we will be showing that:

- the term 'race' has many negative connotations

- 'ethnicity' is a much broader term, emphasising cultural rather than perceived physical differences.

On its own, the term 'race' is a synonym for 'type', which is socially divisive because it suggests that humans have different origins, thus different capacities and abilities. By the 19th century, race had become a biological classification. Foucault argued that once categorisation has taken place it becomes a site of meaning, power and control (usually in its most insidious form). In other words, once you classify you start to judge. Samuel James Morton, by measuring the size of skulls and cranial capacity (measurement of intellect) 'discovered' five 'races', including the Caucasians (white Europeans), who were supposedly superior to the other four races, and so legitimised white domination of black or dark skinned peoples. Likewise, social Darwinist theories, re-articulated by the sociobiologist Van den Berghe and the functionalist Herbert Spencer, argue that those who occupy superior positions do so because they have won the 'genetic' struggle (Darwin's 'survival of the fittest'). It is Herrnstein and Murray's contention that black people hold an inferior position because they have on average a lower IQ score than white people. They conclude that despite improved educational programmes and life opportunities, the cause of social problems is the 'black' gene rather than social environment.

However, there is no scientific basis to race. There is no proven connection between intelligence and brain size. Similarly, IQ is not a good measure for intelligence; tests are socially constructed and besides, only a small percentage of intelligence rests on inheritance. The work of Steve Jones argues that the colour of somebody's skin does not say much about what is under it. Humans possess 50,000 genes and skin colour is only determined by fewer than 10 genes. Jones concludes that there is very little genetic evidence to distinguish people. Behavioural differences cannot be attributed to physical ones.

Sociologists tend to use the term 'ethnicity' because it emphasises cultural factors and differences rather than the 'natural' or genetic. Ethnic identity often arises from self-definition, self-determination and a shared culture and lifestyle. It is not an all-embracing and overarching label; it does not imply that people who share the same colour of skin constitute a homogeneous group, but allows for differences in values and belief systems. However, it is not wholly unproblematic because it implies difference or being an 'other', which often refers to skin colour. For instance, (predominantly white) Irish immigrants are not commonly attributed the status of 'ethnic' group.

2 Racism and racialism

This section will define and determine the differences between racism and racialism.

Miles defines racism as prejudice and holding preconceived ideas about groups of people. Essentially, racism is a way of thinking (ideas and beliefs) about the apparent (but non-existent) biological differences of different 'races'. However, racism is not static, nor is it one-way, but ever-changing and 'practised' by many ethnic groups. Racialism is the 'theory' put into practice; it is the unequal treatment of various racial groups. More often, it is the discriminatory behaviour of the dominant group towards others on the basis of their colour, culture and/or religion. The term 'institutional racism' refers to a set of in-built exclusionary practices (overt and hidden) that protects the advantaged or dominant group. For example, McPherson concluded that the investigation into Stephen Lawrence's murder was hindered by the Metropolitan Police Force's institutional racism.

3 Theories of racism

The practice of discrimination by some people against others is explained in this section by looking at:

- individual racism

- racism at an institutional and political level.

By fusing together the ideas of Freud and Marxism, the Frankfurt School devised the authoritarian personality. Adorno *et al* argued that certain types of early socialisation lead to racist tendencies in individuals. Children who had been brought up in a cold, loveless and disciplinarian manner were more likely to adopt an anxious and rigid outlook on life. In a huge survey they determined that those people who held traditional values – success, industry, competence, physical cleanliness, health, conformity and so on – were most likely to support leaders such as Hitler. Cashmore describes racism as a type of natural conservatism, which surfaces when people defend the established order of things.

The BCCCS (Birmingham Centre of Contemporary Cultural Studies), through the work of Hall and Gilroy, identified a new racism that was endemic in the discourses on ethnicity during the Thatcher administration. Instead of racism based on perceived 'natural' differences, it was based on cultural differences. Hartman and Husbands' content analysis of the mass media showed that newspapers with articles referring to 'race' often focused on 'problem' issues regarding immigration, race relations, crime, legislation and discrimination. Van Dijk showed that incidents involving black people were not described as social unrest, but attributed to black 'bad' behaviour.

 ## Immigration

This section will discuss:

- government legislation regarding immigration

- Marxist, functionalist, new right, Weberian and post-modern theories regarding immigration.

Since the 1948 British Nationality Act allowed *all* citizens of the Commonwealth to enter the UK to work and settle, successive governments have introduced legislation to 'manage' immigration. However, most laws have concentrated on stopping access; immigration by black people has been defined as a 'problem'. These fears were popularised by Enoch Powell in a speech in 1968 in which he said, 'As I look ahead I am filled with foreboding. Like the Roman I seem to see "the River Tiber foaming with much blood".' Immigration policy has been designed to control the numbers of Asian and black immigrants. Popular discourses on immigration focused on the 'threat' to the British way of life by black communities.

Stratification – Ethnicity and Race

Although immigration has been decreasing since the early 1960s, new immigration laws have been commonplace. In 1981, a law demanded that British passport holders resident abroad with no family connections in the UK were denied entry. In 1988, would-be immigrants had to pass an 'independent of public funds test' to show that they could live without applying for benefits. Richer, white immigrants from South Africa and Hong Kong have been welcomed, whereas asylum seekers, many of whom have fled for their lives, are sometimes incarcerated like prisoners. It is forgotten, argue Castles and Miller, that colonialism has created migration. Similarly, Pilkington and Bradley believe that the roots of contemporary divisions between white and black people are derived from European colonialism. As Lawrence points out, the experience of colonising other nations has shaped views on the supposedly 'savage' and 'child-like' characteristics of immigrants.

The functionalist account argues that conflict is derived from cultural differences. If the cultural characteristics of minority groups do not fit into society's traditional norms and values it undermines the social consensus. In other words, immigrants and ethnic minorities have to adapt and conform to the host nation, whilst it remains passive. Assimilation, according to Park, is the most permanent solution; it is much better than accommodation (living and working on friendly rather than harmonious terms) and conflict. Richardson and Lambert criticise the functionalist account for assuming that groups of people will want to surrender their cultural practices and identity. The idea of 'cultural incompatibility' and foreign people's disruptive nature is one that is close to the ideas of the New Right, who have attacked West Indians, for example, for being problematic because they do not accept authority and are prone to criminality (Casey 1982). According to Gilroy, former prime minister Margaret Thatcher's new brand of racism was based on the presumption that British (white) people feared being 'swamped' by people of other cultures. By using a revised definition, the term 'race' was made redundant, so 'racist' agendas could not be racist by definition (even if the discourses were). Norman Tebbitt's 'cricket test' ('Who do you support, England or Pakistan/India/West Indies?') for immigrants was based on the idea that being British could be measured by how you live your life rather than proving your ownership of a British passport.

Marxists argue that the state reproduces the relations of production, resulting in economically stronger countries dominating other countries in the quest for profit. For example, colonies have been used to produce a single product such as coffee (which makes them highly dependent on richer nations for other goods and services). Underdevelopment, typified by the lack of an adequate infrastructure, has forced people to migrate and play a disadvantaged role in the host country. Castles and Kosack (1973) describe immigrants as a reserve army of labour, which serves to fragment the proletariat. Their study of immigration in European countries showed that all immigrants share the same class position. For Cox, class is the primary division in society, but racism and discrimination are actively encouraged to split the working class (divide and conquer). In other words, in addition to being a source of cheap labour, it suppresses wages; it is a form of group control, an ideological construction and by-product of class oppression.

The Weberian discussion on ethnicity is very similar to Marxism. The lower status position of ethnic groups is both ideological and reflects structural realities. Parkin describes the social esteem of ethnic minority groups as 'negatively privileged'. Rex found that black immigrant groups were often housed in poor accommodation because their status as semi-British citizens disqualified them from being the recipients of newer and better housing (simply because they were not on the housing list long enough compared with white people). The situation is worsened because the different ethnic groups compete with each other for limited resources such as housing, employment and education.

The post-modernist account foresees a new social order, in which people will celebrate the diversity of peoples from around the world. It attacks the one-dimensional nature of the theories in traditional sociology. For example, not all black people are 'victims'; many have been active in opposing their subordination. Neither are identities fixed; individuals can pick and choose identities which are no longer dependent on skin colour. Racism can be explained by people's uncertainty; they may feel threatened by changing identities. However, post-modernism probably does not really reflect the every-day experience of racism. By ignoring the objective facts and effects of discrimination, it ignores the very real socioeconomic differences between different ethnic groups.

5 Inequalities in work between ethnic groups

Ethnicity is in itself another stratification system. Black minority groups are disproportionately more likely to be poor. Other factors such as class and sex should not be ignored. This section will review:

- work opportunities for ethnic minority groups

- the responses to discrimination by different ethnic minority groups.

In the labour market, there are straightforward links between the discrimination and prejudice of employers and immigrants' holding lower paid occupations. Brown and Gay's 'application test' project showed that white applicants for jobs were received more positively than black applicants. Rex and Tomlinson describe the lowly position of black people as a consequence of the dual labour market. Immigrants are more likely to be employed in the secondary labour market. The role for black workers, according to Castles and Kosack, is to act as a reserve army of labour.

Cross has shown how some ethnic minority groups have raised their social position. It is argued that some are culturally predisposed for enterprise; they operate in markets for ethnic minorities and respond to discrimination by starting their own businesses. Ballard's comparison of Sikh and Muslim immigration focused on the internal preferences of each group as well as the external constraints. They looked at the point of origin of each group and showed that cultural and regional differences affected skill levels and their ability to adapt. However, Pryce's study showed that Jamaican immigrants adapted in many different ways to immigration. In stark contrast, Murray concluded that black people are simply unwilling to work because they can live on welfare benefits. This has taken away the motivation to work, encouraged the growth in single-parent families and diminished self-responsibility.

45 minutes

Use your knowledge

1 Contrast the biological and cultural differences between different groups of people.

2 How does a person's ethnicity affect their life chances?

3 Describe the sociological explanations of immigration.

Welfare and Poverty

20 minutes

Test your knowledge

1 The aim of the _____ Report was to eradicate the five giants of poverty. They were, _____, _____, _____, _____ and _____. Between 1945 and 1979, governments adopted _____ economic policies to fund these new measures. The most enduring of these institutions have been state education and the _____ _____ Service. The election of the _____ _____ in 1979 marked the end of consensual politics in Great Britain. Instead, the new administration adopted _____ policies – it committed itself to cutting taxes, whilst seeking to introduce a _____ philosophy to public services.

2 New Right theorists, such as _____ and _____ , contest the usefulness of the welfare state. They argue that it creates a _____ culture. The social democratic position is one that argues that the state is morally obliged to _____ to extend the citizenship rights of the whole population. The Marxist account describes the introduction of the welfare state as warding off _____ _____. It acts in the interests of the _____ _____.

3 It has been argued that the welfare state has not _____ poverty. According to _____ it is the middle class that have benefited most, through subsidies for transport, health and education. On the other hand, relatively less well-off people, due to increases in VAT, are now seeing their burden increase. This is known as a _____ tax.

4 Poverty can be defined in one of two ways: _____ poverty is based on what an individual requires to maintain a subsistence level, whereas _____ poverty refers to those who cannot pursue a socially acceptable ordinary life. The most famous exponents of this approach are _____, _____ and _____, authors of Breadline Britain. They showed that, despite the common assertion that poverty had been eradicated, the number of people living in poverty in 1990s Britain was comparable with _____'s study of Victorian Britain.

5 For Marxists, poverty is an inevitable feature of _____ society. _____ _____ theorists argue that poverty is a consequence of individual actions and personal deficiencies.

Answers

1 Beveridge, idleness, squalor, want, disease and ignorance, Keynesian, National Health, Conservative Party (Margaret Thatcher), monetarist, market **2** Murray, Saunders, dependency, intervene, class conflict, ruling class **3** eradicated, Le Grand, regressive **4** absolute, relative, Townsend, Mack and Lansley, Rowntree **5** capitalist, New Right

✔ **If you got them all right, skip to page 40**

Welfare and Poverty

30 minutes

Improve your knowledge

1 The development of the welfare state

The principles of the welfare state were laid down four hundred years ago. This section is concerned with reviewing:

- major changes in the welfare state

- the impact of Thatcherism on welfare state provisions.

The origins of the welfare state can be dated back to the early 17th century, when the Poor Law (1601) was introduced, which had distinct policies for different groups – the deserving (sick) and undeserving (lazy and deviant) poor. The dominant view of poverty was that people were poor because they were lazy and morally, mentally and personally deficient. In 1834 the Poor Law was amended, reflecting the changes in the socioeconomic order. It was acknowledged by progressive political and social theorists that poverty was not necessarily the fault of the poor but might be due to factors outside their control. For example, social surveys by Booth and Rowntree recognised that poverty was derived from unemployment, low wages and old age. In addition, the franchise was extended to working men and subsequent social reforms started to reflect the 'democratic' general will.

The Liberal reforms in the earlier part of the 20th century introduced national insurance and pensions. The First World War reinforced the need for centralised government, showing at the same time that state planning could play an important role in the redistribution of wealth (rather than just the market). The Beveridge Report (1942) proved to be a revolution in economic thinking, proposing that greater state interference was required to achieve greater security and opportunity for the majority of people. Its aim was to banish the five giants of poverty: idleness, squalor, want, disease and ignorance. The following acts were designed to guarantee a minimum standard of living: the Education Act 1944, the National Insurance Act 1945, the National Health Service Act 1946 and the National Assistance Act 1948. It was assumed that Keynesian policies of full employment would underpin these wide-reaching measures and result in the expansion of the economy.

Key points from AS in a Week

Health pages 52–55

Work (unemployment) pages 62–63

Education (new vocationalism) pages 75–76

Welfare and Poverty

The election of the Conservative government in 1979 marked the end of consensual politics in Britain. New Right social policies (see the chapter on Power and Politics for an overview) saw the rejection of the Keynesian commitment to full employment, advocating instead that the market should be left to find the 'natural' rate of employment, whilst people should start taking responsibility for their own welfare. For example, the Thatcher government introduced market approaches to care services; the aim of the internal markets or 'quasi-markets' was to ensure that the public sector operated on the basis of demand, supply and competition, making it more efficient. Schools were also subjected to the principles of competition, through more parental choice, the publication of league tables and funding related to pupil numbers. Individuals were encouraged to arrange provisions for their own private pensions, not least by the reduction in state pensions. Benefit payments became more selective (means-tested), whereas benefits for 16- to 18-year-olds were replaced by training schemes, such as the Youth Opportunity Programme and Youth Training Scheme. Thatcherism also encouraged what it labelled a 'home owning, share owning democracy', selling council houses and privatising public utilities such as British Gas, British Telecom and the Electricity Board. Care was also shifted from institutions into the community and family.

These policies, designed to relieve the burden (or so-called crisis) of the welfare state, were coupled with a commitment to reduce income tax and encouragement of private wealth. However, they did not result in a commensurate increase in take-home pay. As Burchardt and Hills showed, private welfare provisions cost individuals the equivalent of a six pence rise in income tax. Furthermore, despite a commitment to reduce expenditure on the welfare state, it remained relatively constant throughout the Thatcher administration. It has been argued by critics such as Hutton that these reforms were ideologically rather than economically motivated. Unfortunately, as Booth and Rowntree had noted over a century ago, when left to its own devices, the market is not a very good provider of health, universal education and housing. For instance, the 'care in the community' policies were supposed to make care more responsive, whilst taking the strain off the state. Unfortunately, care was not guaranteed; it was unequally provided, under-funded and the agencies were not publicly accountable. Some critics have suggested that the de-institutionalisation of mental patients has resulted in the increase in homelessness.

Welfare and Poverty

 Ideologies and theories of welfare

There are broadly three schools of thought regarding the role of the welfare state. They are:

- the New Right perspective, which argues that state interference should be minimal

- the social-democratic approach, which proposes that the welfare state is beneficial to the wealth of the nation

- the Marxist account, which describes it as a tool of class oppression.

As noted in the section above, it is the belief of the New Right that the market is better than the state at providing services because society is far too complex for the state to provide everything in adequate amounts. In *The Road to Serfdom*, Hayek argued that a wide-reaching welfare state discouraged individualism, independence and self-reliance and allowed the 'evil' of socialism to creep in through the back door. The book also had a strong moralistic edge: people must bear the responsibility of their own actions rather than be protected against misfortune. It is thought that welfare creates a culture of dependency rather than self-reliance, therefore creating a spiral of poverty. Right-wing theorists such as Saunders and Murray argue that it has not only allowed, but encouraged single-parent families to develop, which are at the heart of a burgeoning and dangerous underclass.

The social-democratic position is much more egalitarian. The state is obliged to eradicate want and suffering; if it can centralise economic planning, it can also centralise social planning. It is seen as essential that all aspects of citizenship should be equal amongst all. Not only do people have individual rights that should be upheld (e.g. freedom of speech), they also have political rights (e.g. being politically active) and social rights (e.g. education). Expenditure on welfare can also be seen as a form of investment. For example, an educated workforce makes a country more economically competitive in the world market. It also builds a collective consciousness and a commitment to society.

The Marxist approach is highly critical of the welfare state because it stabilises and reproduces capitalism by offering concessions to the working class. It works on two levels; firstly, it wards off class conflict by 'diluting' the true horror of capitalism. As Offe points out, the welfare state may have improved working-class conditions but it has reduced working-class militancy by reducing the harsher effects of exploitation. Secondly, according to Ginsburg, benefits are kept low, so that wages may be suppressed as well. The fear of relying on benefits also acts to discipline people to the work ethic. O'Connor sees the welfare state as 'dysfunctional' because it undermines people's confidence in a system which should, but cannot, provide for increasing expectations. This is what Habermas described as a legitimation crisis which ends in social crisis and disturbances. Feminists regard welfare policies such as the Beveridge Report as sexist and a reinforcement of women's dependency on men, citing their lack of eligibility for benefits and lack of provisions such as comprehensive childcare.

 ## Who benefits from the welfare state?

The central questions for social theorists are:

- Who actually benefits from the provisions of the welfare state?

- Does the welfare state really promote greater equality or is it a system of stratification in itself?

The welfare state was introduced to act as a safety net but it is argued that it creates a distinction between those who work and those receiving benefit (i.e. those who are poor). For Esping-Anderson it promotes social 'dualisms'. Rather than eradicate inequalities, welfare has maintained them. Having liberal approaches to social policy, coupled with a growing middle class and private provisions, has undermined the notion of 'universality'. In essence, it has served to maintain class and status differences. Benefits are stigmatised because they tend to be low, whilst complicated rules and regulations discourage people from claiming. Furthermore, Le Grand (1982) showed that the middle class benefit most from welfare provisions, such as health, education, public transport and social services. For example, middle-class children are more likely to continue and further their education and so funds are directed towards those groups rather than those who most need it. This further exacerbates the dual nature of society. According to Bryson (1992), women have not benefited because it has been assumed that they should be male-dependent, and as a consequence, excluded by work and factory acts. This is what Williams calls the gendered construction of welfare. It is described as a double bind: on one hand it improves women's conditions, whilst on the other it condemns them to a secondary position, by 'blocking' women from fully participating in the labour market. By making the receiving of benefits reliant on contributions from paid employment, the welfare state automatically discriminates against those disadvantaged in the labour market. In particular, due to discrimination and racism, workers from ethnic minority backgrounds have been employed in lower paid jobs, which have resulted in lower contributions.

Central to the philosophy of the welfare state is the notion that the redistribution of income can be achieved through progressive taxation (the rich pay proportionately more tax), whilst regressive taxation should be avoided. However, by shifting the burden of taxation from people's income (based on the ability to pay, rather than a flat rate) to expenditure, the Thatcher administration moved the tax burden onto the poor. Taxes for the highest earners were cut significantly. For example, the top band of income tax was reduced from 60% to 40%, whilst VAT was increased from 7% to 17.5%. A higher proportion of poor people's income is spent on everyday necessities (such as food, clothing, bills). Effectively, their tax burden became greater. In contrast, those with money to save or invest in property enjoyed tax relief. In many cases, the better-off also enjoyed share schemes and other fringe benefits (such as private health and company cars). For many critics, therefore, the welfare state, or more specifically, the management of the welfare state, has encouraged inequality. The Child Poverty Action Group calculated that the benefits received by someone earning £40,000 a year were only £1 less than those received by an unemployed person.

Similarly, changes in the economy, i.e. de-industrialisation, had a profound and lasting effect, culminating in hundreds of thousands of job losses. Since 1979, unemployment doubled but it has been unequally experienced. As Oppenheim and Harker show, a construction worker is ten times more likely to be made unemployed than a middle-class professional. Increased unemployment coupled with benefit cuts reduced the income of the bottom 10%. Although share ownership increased, it was the richest 1% who benefited most – they own 75% of the shares (Scott, 1994).

The functionalist position on inequality describes it as functional because it ensures that the most talented people are encouraged to take on the most important positions in society (Davis and Moore). For Saunders, it is inevitable that societies are unequal, which acts as a motivating force. People are rational, they are encouraged to make money and in doing so, they make the economy richer, which 'trickles down' and benefits the rest of society by providing work. However, who and what determines which occupations are more important and functional than others? It assumes that those who are paid most are more functional – is this really the case?.

For Marxists, inequality is a product of exploitation. People are poor because others are rich. The rich are rich because they live off the work of others. There is nothing natural or inevitable about inequality and as the working class becomes increasingly aware and disenchanted with their exploitation, the working-class consciousness will strengthen and eventually overthrow capitalism.

 ## 4 Poverty

Although the welfare state was set up to eradicate poverty, it remains. This section will concentrate on:

- definitions of poverty

- competing theories of poverty.

There are two definitions of poverty: absolute poverty and relative poverty. People are living in absolute poverty when they have insufficient funds for basic necessities: adequate food, clothing and shelter. Rowntree's study of poverty in York in 1883 found that 28% of people were living in absolute poverty. However, in Britain today, absolute poverty is rare. Relative poverty is not just based on survival but measures the ability to live a normally active life in society. If people cannot afford an adequate (balanced) diet or are unable to engage in ordinary activities which are customary, they are according to this definition 'poor'. Townsend devised a 'deprivation' index, which measured how poor people really are. He calculated that where household incomes were less than 140% of the 'supplementary benefit' level, people had to do without. Poverty, according to Townsend, can only be defined objectively when it is applied relatively. This was the basis of research conducted in the 1950s and 1960s, which asked if poverty had really been eradicated. As Bradshaw reminds us, relative poverty is not just about lifestyle; there are definite health implications as well. Families living on supplementary benefit, and forced to buy the cheapest lines, fell 6500 calories short a week, as well as being deficient in many essential nutrients, such as calcium and fibre.

Absolute poverty is a more understandable and universal definition, which tends to fit into everyday ideas of poverty; for example, it formed the basis of the Beveridge Report. However, if absolute poverty changes, can it be absolute? Also, in some countries is it still a useful, indeed moral form of classification to compare others against? Relative poverty accepts that poverty is a social construction and allows for variations from region to region, which reflects the cultural, economic and environmental diversity of lifestyles. It is criticised for being arbitrary; who decides what should be included in the criteria? New Right theorists argue that it is a measure of inequality not poverty and it moves the 'level' of poverty upwards. It assumes that people behave identically. What if people chose to adopt a lifestyle (e.g. vegetarian) that is, according to Townsend *et al*, 'deprived'? It is best to see poverty as involuntary multiple deprivation; ranging from inadequate educational opportunities, unpleasant working conditions and lack of money to powerlessness. Poverty implies a shortfall in material and cultural resources.

Sociologists such as Bradshaw, who are concerned with studying poverty, have shown, by using Rowntree's original definition of absolute poverty, that poor people in Britain today are less well-off when compared with people at the turn of the century. The Breadline Britain study by Mack and Lansley using a relative definition concluded similarly; poverty was more prevalent than the authorities had estimated. Their study is methodologically interesting because the respondents devised a list of what they thought was important to live a normal life. According to their study (1990), they found that 11 million people were living in poverty, whilst 5 million could not afford fresh food, whereas 'luxuries' (treats, hobbies, etc.) were not available to 21 million people. By establishing a consensual view of what people considered to be an acceptable standard of living, they showed in 1990 that 7.5 million people did not have access to three or more necessities, whereas 3.5 million were regarded as being severely poor by lacking seven or more necessities. Since 1983, relative and severe poverty had increased in the so-called 'booming 80s'. The groups most likely to fall into these categories were low-paid workers, single parents, the sick and disabled and pensioners.

However, a poverty-line in the UK has never been officially recognised. John

Moore, former Secretary of State for Social Security, argued that 'want' had been eliminated. Despite this assertion, more people were poor during the Conservative administration than before. For example, between 1979 and 1993, the richest 10% increased their income by 62%, whereas the income of the poorest 10% fell by 17%. The Joseph Rowntree Foundation (1995) also showed that income inequality had worsened since the 1970s. In addition, official unemployment had reached figures not seen since the Great Depression of the 1930s.

 ## Theories explaining poverty

This section is specifically concerned with the different theoretical approaches to explaining why poverty occurs. Broadly it will concentrate on:

- structural approaches that recognise that poverty is a product of economic/political arrangements

- the belief that poverty can be attributed to individual deficiencies.

The social-democratic perspective describes unemployment as a very real objective fact – if there are no jobs, what are people to do? It is the labour market and unemployment that leads to poverty. This position stipulates that people are victims rather than architects of their own downfall and if the market is left to its own devices it cannot produce sufficient welfare. For example, changes in the labour market have resulted in less opportunities for people to remove themselves from unemployment and poverty. Poverty continues to exist despite the welfare state, through the failure of the market to redistribute wealth adequately.

The Marxist approach to poverty describes it as a permanent feature of capitalism, because it does not serve people's needs. The reserve army keeps wages low, which increases surplus value and profit. All capitalist systems develop welfare not to eliminate poverty but to ensure the poor can physically survive, because capitalism causes fundamental social problems.

Individualistic approaches to poverty blame the behaviour and culture of the poor; they are responsible for their situation. The Conservatives individualised poverty, implying that the poor had a weakness of a physical, mental or moral kind. There is a culture of poverty which regenerates itself through inadequate parenting and home background. New Right thinkers, such as Marsland and Murray argue that a dependency culture exists; the poor receive an income for doing nothing, which acts as a disincentive to work. Murray complains that despite massive improvements in living standards and the introduction of welfare programmes, the poor have become poorer. He berates the poor for being inadequate individuals and creating an inadequate culture. This echoes the work of Spencer, who believed it to be unnatural to help those who led 'dissolute lives' and not to allow them to experience the consequence of their actions. It was their lack of moral character that caused their suffering.

Despite the prevalence of these opinions in popular discourses about poverty, there have been many critical responses to those who blame the poor for their predicament. In stark contrast to Marsland, Jordan believes that universal benefits are essential. If people had to pay for their education and health, it would only exacerbate their economic and social situation. In addition, Dean and Taylor-Gooby point out that the New Right critics conveniently 'forget' that we are all dependent on the state in one form or another (for example, on the police for physical security). From this point of view, the benefit claimant is no more dependent on the state than others.

Neglecting to understand the situation from the point of view of people experiencing poverty has also led to gross over-generalisation and simplification of many people's financial and social situation. For example, the poor are constrained by the situation they find themselves in, and their values may not be so different from those of the middle class; they do not have the means to realise them. Culturally, the middle class may be superior and should be congratulated on their ability to defer gratification but the poor cannot defer it if there is nothing to defer in the first place! For Bourdieu, it may be that poorer people have a more realistic outlook on life.

45 minutes

Use your knowledge

1. How have New Right theories contributed to an understanding of the nature and distribution of poverty?

2. Has the welfare state been successful in eliminating the two 'giants' of want and ignorance?

3. Describe and account for the different approaches to measuring poverty.

4. Can public provisions be adequately made by non-governmental bodies?

Power and Politics

Test your knowledge

1 Weber distinguishes between _____ , which can be defined as imposing one's will over another, and _____ , which is exercised when the people accept the right for others to tell them what to do. The functionalist account, described by _____ , is known as the _____-_____ model. The _____ view is known as the zero-sum model, because power is _____. Gramsci coined the term _____ , to describe how people consented to their subordination. According to Miliband a cohesive _____ rules. Similarly, Mills describes the _____ _____ who run America for their benefit and not society's.

2 The nation-state is probably the most legitimate form of power in the world. Marxists believe that the state serves the interests of the _____ _____. The earliest writers in the liberal tradition stressed the necessity of the state. For Rousseau, the state's role was to override the particular will and serve the _____ will. Nazi Germany and Stalinist Russia are examples of what Friedrich defined as _____ _____. In the West, _____ is the most prevalent political system today.

3 Liberalism emphasises _____ and _____ state interference to ensure liberty. The _____ provides what people want rather than what it thinks they want. Amongst other things, the Conservatives are opposed to _____ , preferring evolution. They believe that social hierarchies are natural and also advocate a strong _____. The 1980s marked a rejection of _____ _____. Conservatism had adopted the policies of the _____ _____ , based on the work of Hayek and Friedman, emphasising _____ and political _____. _____ emphasises cooperation rather than competition. Socialist-democratic parties believe in the _____ of wealth from rich to the poor through taxation.

4 Interest groups do not seek to gain _____ but to exert pressure. The _____ account refers to the participation of many groups in the political process. Pressure groups, such as the CBI are known as _____. The BMA is an example of a _____ group, representing the interests of doctors. _____ pressure groups enjoy a much more privileged position because of their expertise.

5 Research into voting behaviour during the 1950s and 1960s focused on _____ _____ and _____. It was believed that the _____ _____ voted Labour, whereas the _____ _____ voted Conservative. However, recent research has focused on _____ _____ ; people feel less attached to their traditional parties.

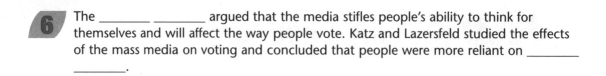
6 The _____ _____ argued that the media stifles people's ability to think for themselves and will affect the way people vote. Katz and Lazersfeld studied the effects of the mass media on voting and concluded that people were more reliant on _____ _____.

Answers

1 power, authority, Parsons, variable-sum, Marxist, power, finite, hegemony, elite, power elite 2 ruling class, general, totalitarian states, democracy 3 freedom, minimal, market, revolution, nation, consensual politics, New Right, economic, freedom, Socialism, redistribution 4 power, pluralist, consultancies, sectional, insider 5 party identification, loyalty, working class, middle class, partisan dealignment 6 Frankfurt School, opinion leaders.

 If you got them all right, skip to page 56

Power and Politics

40 minutes

Improve your knowledge

Explanations for the nature and distribution of power

Key points from AS in a Week

Socialisation (class) pages 17–19

Mass media (audiences) pages 41–45

This section will look at the competing theories on how power is distributed in society. This will include:

- a discussion of the dominance of liberal democratic theories of power

- a critique of 'democracy' by Marxist theorists.

Weber described power as the ability to impose one's will on another (including force). According to Weber, stark, aggressive power is rare in modern societies. Weber defined authority as people accepting the right of others to tell them what to do. This is what Weber labelled as legitimate power. He suggested that there are three types of authority. Charismatic power is derived from a person's exceptional qualities. Martin Luther King was a highly charismatic leader of the Civil Rights Movement. Power based on traditional authority demands that the holders of office should be obeyed because they always have been obeyed. An example of this is the 'divine right' to rule of kings and queens. The legal-rational model is the one that is most prevalent in the liberal-democratic Western world today. The population knowingly and willingly transfers and entrusts power to another group to achieve specific goals (for example, the collection of taxes, funding and allocating resources for economic management, welfare, defence and law and order).

There are many competing theoretical accounts to explain how power is distributed. The functionalist perspective, espoused by Parsons, is known as the variable-sum model. According to Parsons, power is infinite and can expand and contract according to its legitimacy. For example, money is, for all intents and purposes, a bit of paper and has no inherent value – its value is based on our belief in it. If we suspect that our five-pound note is a forgery, we will probably feel reluctant to hand it over for the exchange of goods because it will not be accepted. Political power is the same; the less people believe in the right of the power-holders, the less power they will have (and vice versa). As Dahl points out, elections are a form of social control, which make representative elites answerable to the electorate. Once a political party loses credibility, they can no longer legitimately exercise power. The premise of functionalist thought is that power is given by the collective will of the people. Furthermore, political parties appeal to a broad range of people by representing the major social groups. Their political ideologies, although they undergo changes (e.g. New Labour), reflect the material interests of those they draw support from. For example, the Conservative Party is a party of tradition, whereas the Labour Party believes in progressive change and reform. Despite what would appear to be a convergence between the two parties, they are ideologically different.

In contrast, the Marxist view of power, is described as the zero-sum model. Marxists argue that power is finite, it can only be held by one person or group at any one time, hence the class struggle. Authority is a disguised form of power. The working class, through a number of ideological and repressive state apparatuses are 'persuaded' that the position of the power-holders is legitimate and in the interests of all. Although the majority of people are 'enslaved' by capitalism, the majority support it. Why is this so?

According to Gramsci, ideological forces affect the way people see and think about capitalism and how it excludes other options. The organic nature of *hegemony* (one group having power over another) allows it to be remarkably inviting in that it includes and it dilutes, at the same time, resistance and conflict. However, whilst students will recognise that there are many competing points of view on how the political, economic and social world should be organised, in reality many are not seen as viable alternatives. They are seen as 'peculiar' ideas confined to one extreme or another (for example, Marxism). Hegemony exists through the consent of the people; by having elections, the people ostensibly legitimise the social, political and economic arrangements.

This is a re-evaluation of 'classic' Marxist thinking, articulated by Hirst, who describes the type of democracy we know today as not 'real' democracy but bourgeois democracy. As Marx wrote, the state is 'but a committee for managing the common affairs of the bourgeoisie' (*The Communist Manifesto*). This implies that it is capitalists who rule, not 'sovereign' parliaments and political governments. Miliband is the main proponent of the single and cohesive upper class thesis. He argues that the most senior members of the 'elite' in state and government are interconnected by family ties, ownership of business and their attendance at 'Oxbridge'. For example, many Conservative MPs are also multiple directors of companies, which leads Miliband to conclude that this 'elite' rules the state for their own interests. Giddens (although not a Marxist) concludes similarly, showing that those who hold powerful positions, for example in finance and industry, are predominantly from public school backgrounds.

In response to Miliband, Poulantzas offered a structural interpretation. He argued that the state is not necessarily under the direct control of one group; it just happens that it always acts in their interests, even if not deliberately. This allows for a degree of relative autonomy by the state. However, the cultural assumptions of the staff (civil service) who make decisions on a day-to-day basis support the status quo. Therefore, the class composition of the 'ruling class' is not important. In addition, because capitalism is international, the opportunity for socialist governments to individually halt capitalism is limited. It would cause a major economic crisis and failure would be certain.

Offering a conflict perspective, Lukes (in *Power: A Radical View*) argues that power, or the exercise of power by elite groups, can be seen on three levels. First, power is based on the ability to make decisions. Second, power is exercised by groups who can set the agenda. Powerful groups can avoid making decisions by ignoring or preventing discussions about certain issues. Third, Lukes proposes that power is exercised invisibly by manipulating the wishes of subordinate groups, by shaping their perceptions of the world through different agencies (for example, education, the media, etc.). This position echoes the work of Gramsci, by emphasising the supportive power of 'normality' and common-sense approaches to thinking about the world.

Mills in *The Power Elite* criticises American politics by questioning its democratic credentials. According to Mills, it is characterised by the activities of three unrepresentative elites: the economic, political and military elites, and together they run the country for their own benefit. The relative power of each varies according to the most pressing political and economic circumstances. For example, during the Cold War, the military elite was the most powerful and thus influential in formulating American policy. The problem for Mills is that the elite's interests are not the same as the real interests of the people. Therefore, resources are misdirected, and Congress is rendered powerless actually to change or achieve anything. The knock-on effect on society is very grave; it leaves the middle class to compete with one another, whilst the working class become de-radicalised and uncritical of the social structures that condemn them to their lowly position, preferring to (and to an extent, having to) concentrate on survival. As a consequence, the activities of the elite go unquestioned.

The classic elite theorists, namely Mosca and Pareto, sought to explain how and why different elites came to power. The implication of this position is that ruling elites are desirable, natural and inevitable. Mosca defined superior groups as those people who were better organised and coordinated to maintain control. In *The Circulation of Elites*, Pareto suggested that different epochs require different types of leaders; some circumstances require 'lions' (those who will use violence), whereas others require 'foxes' (who use negotiation and manipulation).

 ## Power and the state

This section is primarily concerned with:

- defining the state's role in modern society

- the 'classic' theories of the state.

Dunleavy and O'Leary define the state as having the following features. First, it is separate from civil society; there are distinct public and private spheres. Second, it is sovereign; it has the right to self-determination, making laws, rules and regulations in its own geo-political space. This echoes Weber's contention that the state also has the legitimate right to use coercion and violence. Third, the state treats all people equally. In practice, the state should be completely neutral by serving whoever is in government. Fourth, it is run by a bureaucracy, a hierarchy of trained people known as civil servants. The agencies of the state have the ability to raise taxes.

Many theorists have contested how and why the state emerged. The major debate has been between the Marxist and liberal traditions. For Engels, the origins of the state lie in the creation of private property and the need to manage class conflict in the interests of the ruling class. From this point of view, especially for Marx, the state is an admittance that we do not have the same interests. If we did have the same interests we would not require it. However, the liberal tradition argues that the state developed out of self-interest (i.e. moving from a state of nature). As Held points out, the work of early political theorists, such as Hobbes is a 'decisive contribution to the formation of the liberal tradition' (1987: 50). Hobbes' *Leviathan* (1651) described the necessity of the state, claiming that without it, life would be 'solitary, poor, nasty, brutish and short' (Oakshott, 1960: 82). According to Hobbes, the most important role for the state is to provide security, which requires compliance from all people, otherwise people would return to the 'state of nature' or civil war and the 'not-so-noble savage' (re: Rousseau). Hobbes wrote, 'Men *(sic)* have no pleasure, but on the contrary a great deal of grief ... where there is no power to overawe them all.' (Oakshott 1960: 81) Hobbes' work was revolutionary because it broke from traditional conceptions of the association between a public body that served the community and civil society. Whilst there is security, it was argued, people would remain loyal to the state (after all it was in their interest). However, if that security is no longer provided by the state, the obligation is broken, people have the 'right', as they do in America, to bear arms so that they may resist oppression.

Another early political theorist, Rousseau, contrived the notion of popular sovereignty or social contract. In other words, there had to be agreement amongst all. This marked a more participatory approach to democracy. For Rousseau, freedom was about overriding the particular will and conforming to the general will, even if it is contrary to your own opinion. To use Rousseau's principles in a contemporary setting one could look towards the pro-hunting lobby as an example of people ignoring the general will. Similarly, John Locke's conception of the state was that the government, through the state, was an instrument to protect, 'life, liberty and estate'. Like Hobbes, he argued that in the 'state of nature' people do not have obligations or duties to one another. The state of nature has to be 'managed', and like Rousseau, he argued that political participation is the route to freedom.

Around the world, nation states take many different forms, and many do not aspire to granting the freedoms envisaged by Locke, and to some extent Rousseau. Nazi Germany and Stalin's Russia, despite having very different political ideologies, are thought of as examples of totalitarian states. These types of political systems boast an ideology (National Socialism and Communism respectively) that embraces everybody, a single party led by a dictator, the employment of terror and violence to gain compliance and complete control of all economic and social institutions (Friedrich, 1954). On the other hand, democracy, or rule by the people, is championed as the antithesis of the totalitarian state. There are many variations of democracy, and despite its ancient Greek origins as *the* defining legitimate political system, it has only recently come into widespread use. Thinkers such as Fukuyama argue that a global consensus has arrived, and that the world is being Westernised. However, the strong resurgence of Islamic states suggests that the process is far from complete. Marxists describe this process as Americanisation, where new markets are forged for the 'American' way of life and its products.

Despite its ubiquity, Marxist critics such as Bottomore believe that true democracy does not and cannot exist. The capitalist class are the real power brokers because they own the means of production. Likewise, Lash and Urry (1987) describe the undermining effect of disorganised global capitalism. In many instances, the capitalist class call the tune; they can even dictate the nature of national policy. Weber also forewarned about the limits of democracy in modern states, arguing that with the growth of party machines and bureaucracies, the danger was that 'real' choice would be narrowed and the direct influence of people diluted. American politics can already be characterised as being limited in scope, whereas British politics are showing similar signs of convergence between the two main political parties. Democracy, or more specifically, its organisation, has its anomalies too. In many cases, the British first-past-the-post system allows a minority government to rule (the winning party has not actually secured a majority, either in terms of the proportion of those who actually voted or including those who did not).

Political parties and ideologies

The association of the term ideology with totalitarian regimes has given it negative connotations. However, it can be used in two distinct ways:

- There is the Marxist usage of it, describing it as a false body of ideas that masks the true nature of the exploitative relations of capitalist societies.

- Alternatively, we can apply a more general definition: a set of ideas and beliefs that offers meanings to understand the world. The starting point of each theory is an understanding of human nature.

The three main parties have distinct ideological roots. The liberal tradition is associated with the work of Locke, Bentham, Mills and Smith. Liberalism emphasises individualism and minimal state interference in people's lives to ensure liberty. Liberals argue that humans are rational and will always seek those things that give pleasure, hence the importance of market forces in determining the distribution of goods and services; the market provides what people want rather than what it thinks they want.

The philosophy of Burke is associated with Conservatism. Conservatives are opposed to revolution, preferring evolution instead – it is less traumatic for all when society changes itself slowly or adapts to new circumstances. Conservatism also advocates strong nationhood, which is based on long-held traditions that have evolved and stood the test of time – for example, the belief that social hierarchies are natural and inevitable; some people are born to lead. Conservatism tends to have a negative view of human nature – people's 'badness' needs to be controlled, hence their emphasis on law and order.

For many commentators, Margaret Thatcher's adoption of free-market policies fused together with traditional Conservatism heralded a new political dawn known as Thatcherism. The 1980s marked a rejection of consensual politics, which had characterised British politics since 1945. It was replaced by the ideology of the New Right, which was based on the work of Hayek and Friedman, emphasising economic and political freedom; the market rather than the state determines the allocation of goods and services (market morality). The market philosophy ('the disciplines of the market') was brought to bear on the internal dynamics of the National Health Service and state education. In addition to the rejection of Keynesian policies of economic management, Thatcherism was also a rejection of the permissive or 'progressive' culture of the 1960s and 1970s. Thatcher's aim was to clear away the debris of socialism, and privatisation ensued; she wanted to establish a share-holding and home-owning democracy (by selling off council houses). Other measures included the dismantling of trade union power (re: crushing the miners' strike, banning trade unions at GCHQ); cutting income taxes and the privatisation of nationalised industries. Thatcher's legacy is a political and economic environment that is near impossible to turn around. For example, if any government wanted to re-nationalise once publicly-owned industries, it would be economically, legally, politically and socially difficult. To think of Thatcher's administration as a calculated ideological movement is flawed; anecdotal evidence suggests that Thatcher governed with an iron *whim* rather than the iron will. Hall concludes that Thatcherism was a reactionary and nationalistic movement which took on the insidious characteristics of state-sponsored racism and jingoistic attitudes towards foreign countries.

Socialism assumes that people are essentially good – it is society that makes them act badly. Capitalism is the root of all evils, it brings out the worst in people because it is an aggressive and destructive ideology, an environment that creates poor living conditions, poverty and lives of despair. Socialism emphasises cooperation rather than competition. Socialist-democratic parties believe in the redistribution of wealth from rich to poor through taxation and redirecting funds towards national welfare policies. They believe that once economic equality is achieved, other equalities will follow. The appeal and popularity of New Labour has, for some traditional Labour Party members, been indicative of its movement away from its socialist principles. It could be argued that there has been some convergence between the policies of New Labour and the Conservative Party. For example, at the heart of Labour policy was the commitment to public ownership of all major or strategic utilities ('Clause 4') but this was abolished in favour of a 'light-touch' regulation, inherited from the Conservatives.

4 Pressure groups

Interest groups, according to Jean Blondel, 'differ from political parties by their aim, which is not to take power but only to exert pressure' (1969). This section will be examining the following:

- the role of pressure groups

- pressure group activity.

Pluralism, which is inextricably connected with the functionalist position, refers to the meaningful participation and the role of many groups in the political process, most notably pressure groups and political parties. Today, interest groups are seen as essential to the democratic process. As Grant (1989) suggests, representative democracy allows very little participation in the political process. Democracy cannot exist on voting alone; voting has become an isolated and somewhat limited form of participation. Pressure groups, on the other hand, encourage participation. They allow groups of people who feel under-represented to seek alternative, legitimate ways to put forward their point of view. Pressure groups are responsive to changing circumstances; they have an educational function and they make issues public.

Pressure group activity can be divided according to aims, organisation, membership and methods of 'lobbying'. Consultancies, such as trades unions, represented collectively as the TUC (Trades Unions Council), have a close alliance with the Labour Party, whilst the CBI (Confederation of British Industry), which represents the interests of business, is associated with the Conservative Party (although its role weakened during the Thatcher years). Obviously, a strong class division can be identified in these particular pressure groups. These groups are also known as sectional: members share a common interest – in this case, occupation (or class). The BMA (British Medical Association) is also a sectional group, representing the interests of doctors.

Those groups concerned with promoting a particular cause are known as promotional groups. For example, Amnesty International, via the media, seeks to obtain favourable publicity for its campaign to end the imprisonment, torture and execution of 'prisoners of conscience'. These groups can be distinguished from *ad-hoc*, single-issue groups who seek publicity through public demonstrations. Tactics of civil disturbance are usually employed by the economically weakest groups, such as road protesters. In stark contrast, insider pressure groups, such as the UKAEA (United Kingdom Atomic Energy Authority) enjoy a much more privileged position because of their expertise. Hired lobbying groups are professional organisations paid to persuade members of Parliament to adopt or represent a particular view. New social movements are distinct, non-institutionalised groups who offer alternative ideologies and ways of living – for example, New Age travellers. Inglehart (1990) argues that they are more about non-material political issues – such as identity and lifestyle (e.g. consumption preferences, dress). It is Habermas' contention that new social movements are a rational response to the 'failure' of the welfare state. There has been a realisation that the mixed economy cannot, or does not, provide social welfare.

Critics of the pluralist account argue that it overlooks some important factors. Many pressure groups do not have any impact; they do not redress the balance of power in any way. Many pressure groups simply do not have enough resources and contacts to compete with others. It seems that it is those groups with the best resources that are most influential, rather than those groups who win the argument. Therefore some groups, as argued by Lukes, are more powerful than others at setting the agenda. Many groups, for example the unemployed, are unable to organise themselves effectively, but nevertheless they still have a very powerful collective argument. Right-wing critics argue that pressure groups lead to weak government because the government constantly has to bow to them, giving rise to erratic government policies, a phenomenon known as 'policy drift'.

Voting behaviour

This section will deal with the highly complex and problematic sociological issue of voting behaviour. As Adrian Howells used to comment, tongue firmly in cheek, 'Why is it that whoever I vote for, the government always gets in?'. We will be examining competing theories to explain:

- voting and class loyalty

- voting and consumerist/rational choice models.

There are many questions that need to be asked when trying to understand the way that people vote. The task is made more difficult because there are so many competing accounts that respond to every new election. For example, do people still vote according to class? If so, why? If not, why has this pattern changed and how can we account for these changes?

British voters have traditionally been regarded as voting on the basis of social class. For example, the party identification and social class model of the 1950s and 1960s regarded class structures and voting behaviour as relatively stable. The working class has supported the Labour Party; the middle and upper class the Conservatives, whilst the Liberals have gained and enjoyed the support of the middle class. Butler and Stokes argued that people were politically socialised to develop a long-term attachment to a particular party.

On this basis alone, one could assume that elections are a foregone conclusion. Quite clearly, if the numerically larger working class always voted Labour, they should have won all elections. The fact that they have not suggests that the notion of the deviant voter is not a new one. Engels' unconnected but nevertheless pertinent comments about the working class summarise the frustration of Marxists who argue that class is an objective reality. He wrote, 'Once again the British working class has disgraced itself'. So who are these people who disgrace and betray their class? Mckenzie and Silver identified deferential voters (the 'cap-in-hand', 'know-my-place' working class), who see others, typically Conservative politicians, as naturally 'superior' and born to rule.

On the other hand, it may be that a person's subjective class position is different to their objective one. However, this implies that 'proper' voting is aligned to one's class interests. Could it be argued that the term 'deviant voter' has now lost its relevance? Is 'deviant' voting a normal practice? For example, Parkin turns deviant voting on its head by asking if the working class is *really* deviant if they vote Conservative? Parkin describes Britain as a conservative nation, so how is it that people resist this all-encompassing cultural force? Because people are cut off from the dominant values of society (for example, living in established communities like coal-mining), they are more likely to vote for Labour.

From the mid-1970s, sociologists have tended to argue that people no longer vote according to their class position, which is also known as partisan de-alignment. Crewe, in his analysis, argued that fewer voters felt attached to their 'traditional' parties. Likewise, Robertson proposes that the ideological divisions which separated the classes have weakened because of the changing financial circumstances of the working classes, especially those in the south, who have become more affluent, property-owning and more likely to vote Conservative. In addition, fewer people are employed in manual work. Traditional industries and their working-class communities have been fragmented by technical, political and global economic changes, as has membership and power of the trades unions (linked with the Labour Party).

Which party has benefited most from de-alignment? The 'embourgeiosement' of the working class and eighteen years of Conservative rule (between 1979 and 1997) would tend to suggest that the Conservatives, along with the Liberals, benefited most. However, the structure of the electoral system (first-past-the-post) meant that the Liberals did not enjoy a commensurate return in seats, and thus power in the House of Commons. On the other hand, many commentators have suggested that the number of graduates working in the expanding public sector, plus the growth in ethnic minority communities, will benefit the Labour Party. Marxist thinkers, typically Braverman, believe that the de-skilling of middle-class occupations will create a more conscious and radical 'working class for itself' (Marx).

Marshall and Heath have been particularly virulent about the simple but false dualistic thinking that has been imposed on the working and middle class by sociologists, arguing that within the working class itself there have always been massive divisions. Despite increasing home ownership (especially of ex-council houses), many of the working class would always have voted Conservative anyway (35%). Theorists are guilty of harping back to a fictional 'golden age' of community and togetherness. Heath, in particular, asks whether people really voted out of blind loyalty or whether they voted for parties whose policies happened to fit into their own preferences and social and political agenda. For example, many people vote tactically. Tactical voters tend to vote on the basis of preventing the party they most dislike gaining power, by voting for the next strongest, irrespective of whether they support them or not.

The instrumental or pocket book model of voting has replaced the class-based model to explain voting behaviour. This is what former Labour leader, Neil Kinnock described as 'now and me-ism'. In other words, which party will serve my economic interests best? Following a consumerist model – what does the individual want and how far does the party meet their requirements? The rational choice model described by Himmelweit, Humphreys and Jaegar in *How Voters Decide* draws comparisons between voting and purchasing an item from a shop. Voters 'buy' political brands and ideologies. Dunleavy and Husbands divide the electorate according to their occupation, pursuits and interests (known as 'public/private sector' and 'consumption cleavages') to explain voting behaviour. Those who work in, use and depend on public services are more likely to vote Labour, whilst those who depend on private institutions are more likely to vote Conservative. As Crewe points out, the class position of a doctor employed by the NHS is middle class, but if they feel that the Conservative government is 'running down' the NHS, they will vote for a viable alternative.

 ## 6 The media and voting behaviour

The growing importance of and access to the mass media is seen as another significant factor affecting how people vote. Habermas argued that the mass media's invasion of the public sphere has undermined democracy by negating proper, rational debate, and replacing it with stage-managed events, 'sound bites' and misinformation. The Frankfurt School argued that the mass media pacifies people; it limits their ability to think critically and independently. The implication of this position is that a politically biased mass media will have a profound effect on the way people vote, hence the electoral successes of the Conservative party following the support of the British press. In contrast, Katz and Lazersfeld studied the effects of the mass media on voting and concluded that people were more reliant on opinion leaders who interpreted and filtered the media's coverage.

More than at any other time, political success is linked with people's perceptions of party competence. For instance, the public's perception of the Labour Party in the late 1970s and 1980s was that they were less competent to govern. Compared with the Conservatives, the Labour Party was very late to employ public relations professionals. From 1979 onwards, the Conservatives, aided by media consultants Saatchi and Saatchi, devoted time and resources to the media; Conservative Party conferences were stage-managed (ten-minute standing ovations were common), speeches were written allowing for television editing, whilst interviews were often conducted with 'friendly' interviewers.

The media is also seen as important in setting the political agenda. In previous elections, the media tended to concentrate on issues deemed to be the Conservative Party's strengths – the economy, defence and law and order. In the 1997 election, the media appeared to have set a different political agenda, which focused on issues such as dealing with unemployment and improving the welfare state. New Labour overcame their credibility problem through party leaders John Smith and subsequently Tony Blair. A more professional and media-friendly approach (critics have described New Labour as the party of 'spin') was fused together with diluted socialist principles (e.g. the scrapping of Clause Four). This made the party more appealing to middle England (it won the battle for 'Mondeo Man'). The 1997 election landslide win for Labour (it gained 419 seats compared to the Conservatives' 165) indicated that New Labour had broken away from its past.

Changes in media technology and the increasing fragmentation of media audiences will have a lasting and profound effect on the electorate's access to competing political views. Today, despite the prevalence of multi-channel and niche-driven media markets, most people are still using established channels to survey the world of politics. But if this changes, an optimistic approach suggests it will lead to increasing democratisation, plurality and diversity of opinions. However, with no legal commitment for media owners to present a balanced or impartial picture of events, people may be denied access to competing points of view. Relying on these channels for information may result in simplified and distorted world views (as argued by Habermas).

Power and Politics

45 minutes

Use your knowledge

1 'Pluralism best describes the way in which power is exercised in modern society.' How far do you agree with this statement?

2 What impact does the media have on people's voting behaviour?

3 How has New Right thinking impacted on British politics over the last 20 years?

25 minutes

Test your knowledge

1 Development is calculated by a nation's _____ per capita. Increases reflect improvements in a country's development. Hawthorne argues that the second half of the 20th century was characterised by a _____ _____ _____ , which divided the world into two broad camps.

2 Will Rostow identified _____ _____ of growth, as traditional societies move to the 'age of _____ _____'. Other theorists, such as Kerr and McClelland, look at _____ factors which they believe hinder progress.

3 The Marxist account describes trading and political relationships as _____. Underdeveloped countries have remained underdeveloped because of activities by economically stronger capitalist countries. Friedman and Baur, arguing from a _____ _____ perspective, believe that centralised planning is fundamentally flawed. The liberal democratic perspective, articulated through the _____ Reports, recommends that more favourable prices should be paid for Third-World goods to make competition more equitable.

4 _____ is the term for the increasing cultural, political and economic relationship between disparate societies. Harvey and Giddens describe the compression of _____ and _____ as the catalyst of a new world order.

5 Harris argues that large _____ companies bring many advantages to underdeveloped and developing countries. They bring new technology and equipment, forge new markets, import and nurture expertise and help development. However, critics such as Jenkins believe that they lead to _____ of the work force, rapid urban development (and accompanying problems), environmental costs and lack of democracy. Aid comes in many forms: loans through the _____ , from commercial banks and from non-_____ organisations.

6 Birth rates appear to be falling. _____ _____ rates are also falling and people are living longer. For George, eradicating hunger and poverty requires a more equal distribution of income, which is also associated with _____ decline.

7 Mies (1986) argues that development has created women as a female _____ _____. Illich describes how the pre-industrial '_____ _____ _____' has been converted into patriarchal domination and cruder exploitation.

Answers

1 GDP, global power game 2 five stages, mass consumption, cultural
3 exploitative, free market, Brandt 4 Globalisation, time, space
5 multinational, exploitation, IMF, -governmental 6 Infant mortality, fertility
7 global caste, regime of gender

✔ **If you got them all right, skip to page 66**

World Sociology

 Improve your knowledge

1 **Explanations of development and under-development**

By discussing development and underdevelopment, we will be assessing:

- how development is measured

- the historical background to patterns of development and underdevelopment.

The term development has positive connotations; it is synonymous with the term progress. This reflects a Western liberal-capitalist world view, by measuring development primarily in terms of economic progress, facilitated by technological advancements and improvements in education. Today, economic issues are intertwined with political issues, and 'lesser developed countries' are encouraged to develop Western political traditions of democracy and civil liberties. Moreover, the last two decades have marked the decline of socialism as an ideological force. Despite the apparent victory of capitalism as a global, hegemonic force, the Marxist position views the adoption of capitalism as *the* cause of underdevelopment around the world.

Development is calculated by a nation's gross national product (GDP) per capita; that is, the amount of tradeable value divided amongst the population. It assumes that increases in GDP reflect improvements in a country's development, its people's individual wealth and living standards. However, this form of measurement does not account for services and goods that are not marketed. It also assumes that if more goods are sold and bought, then people enjoy a better life. This ignores the number of externalities (e.g. pollution) that tend to accompany greater consumption. In addition, it presupposes that income is shared equally, which it certainly is not. According to Marxist theory, capitalist economies are, by their very nature, exploitative and only the ruling class will benefit from a nation's wealth.

The political and economic climate of the world today has been shaped by the expansionary policies of the colonising powers and the events leading up to, during and after the Second World War. The impact of these divisions has been profound. For Hawthorne, the second half of the 20th century was characterised

Key points from AS in a Week

Methods and assumptions of the social approach
page 12

Conformity and obedience
pages 12–14

by a global power game, also known as the Cold War. Political and military power was divided into two broad camps: the 'West', led by the United States (NATO) and the 'East' (Warsaw Pact countries led by the USSR). Likewise, economic protectionism, in the form of trading associations reflected political loyalties. GATT (General Agreement on Tariffs and Trade) (later replaced by the World Trade Organisation) and its eastern European bloc equivalent, Comecon, served members' interests by ensuring markets for their goods and services. The USA established itself as a leading player in the monetary system; international trade is conducted in US dollars.

2 Theories of change

Modernisation theory rests upon the assumption that progress measures the transition of a simple society to a complex capitalist system. This section will be concerned with:

- Rostow's economic and technical model for growth
- cultural factors that help and hinder economic and social development.

Rostow's (five) *Stages of Growth* (1960) implies that developing nations follow one path:

- First, traditional society lacks modern science.
- In the second stage, the preconditions for 'take off' are established by developing and applying science.
- The third or 'take off' stage is characterised by a growing economy, which is accompanied by a new political elite.
- Fourth is the 'drive to maturity' by reinvesting in the country's infrastructure (roads, factories, housing, etc.).
- The fifth stage or the 'age of mass consumption' is reached, with an economic shift towards durable consumer goods and services. Also, people begin to enjoy higher incomes, more leisure time and benefit from the development of a welfare state.

According to Rostow, the key factors are economic and technological, but other theorists have looked primarily at cultural factors. Kerr also stresses the importance for developing countries of adopting the compromising nature of Western politics if they are to experience development. The implication of cultural modernist thinking, articulated by McClelland (1961), is that cultural traditions should be removed to facilitate economic development. Like Hoselitz, he argues that if a nation's people lack the 'need' to achieve, economies will stagnate. Parsons and Hoselitz conclude that developing nations must adopt Western values and culture if they are to fulfil their programme of modernisation. Similarly, convergence theorists point to not only the coming together of technology and organisational principles but, in the aftermath of the failed political experiments of fascism and communism, the fact that the world is adopting a uniform world view. If Dahrendorf and Bell are correct, all industrial societies will become alike.

The main criticism of modernisation theory is its ethnocentricity. It does not take into account that people may want to maintain their traditional cultures. It also assumes that lack of development can be attributed to a less developed 'culture' rather than geographic location, natural resources or exploitation by other nations or multinational corporations. Do traditional cultures need to be obliterated to achieve economic and political progress? There are many examples of places where tradition and development go hand in hand (e.g. the 'tiger economies' of Japan and SE Asia). Modernisation theory also presupposes that everybody around the world desires the same things. Clearly, they do not, so why should Western values be imposed on other cultures? Such accounts imply that institutional and technological change impacts on people who are powerless, whereas this is not necessarily true.

3 Sociological perspectives on development and underdevelopment

This section concentrates on the competing accounts that attempt to explain the different patterns of development around the world. We will examine:

- the Marxist account, which describes trading and political relationships as exploitative

- the free-market approach, which argues that central planning hinders development

- the Liberal approach, which advocates political intervention by national and international bodies.

World Sociology

For Marxists, inequality takes place on a global (as well as national) scale. The structure of undeveloped countries has been created by the exploitative pursuits of capitalist countries. Marx predicted the concentration of world markets by a few companies, thus polarising the proletariat and the bourgeoisie. Baran and Sweezy describe how the monopoly position of multinational companies affords them great power and privileges – for example, they can conduct business on their own terms (negotiating tax-breaks and government grants). Although investment by foreign companies is seen as a good thing because it creates employment, companies take profits back out of the country again. It would appear that a world socialism new order is not a viable alternative. However, Warren, espousing classic Marxist thinking, believes that the transition from primitive to capitalist societies is an inevitable move towards socialism. For communism to be realised it *has* to move through these 'epochal' stages, so that the economic condition of the working class in relation to the capitalists worsens and a revolutionary consciousness develops. According to Marx, history is characterised by conflict between two diametrically opposed groups competing for ascendancy.

Frank describes the drive towards development, or more specifically capitalism, as inevitably resulting in domination and exploitation by the West; as a consequence, 'real' development is distorted. A pattern of exploitation takes place, the ruling class of satellite countries invites foreign capital by offering 'favourable' (i.e. exploitative) conditions (low pay, no workers' rights) and, in turn, they exploit the subordinate classes. Profits flow upwards towards the ruling class and outwards and so only a few benefit from this 'progress'. This creates a climate of super-exploitation where companies pay workers less than a subsistence level. Coupled with this is the West's ability to 'create' market prices and levels. This unequal exchange, argues Emmanuel (1972), is a result of goods produced by poor countries for rich counties being undervalued, whereas goods developed by the rich are overvalued. A situation arises where the working class of the metropolis benefits from the exploitation of the satellite's rural working class. The effect is two-fold; it serves to divide the working class on a global scale and it is difficult for individual nations to be isolationist in the world capitalist system. Schuurman concludes that most countries cannot escape from a dependency role because they cannot be self-sufficient.

Friedman and Baur oppose central planning, arguing instead that private enterprise should be left to its own devices to develop countries. For them, development theory, which advocates a centralised planning scheme, is fundamentally flawed. However, evidence contradicts this assertion: Germany, Japan and the 'tiger' economies have experienced state intervention and enjoy comparable living standards to the USA.

A large gap between rich and poor, according to the liberal-democratic perspective, also makes countries susceptible to extreme ideologies and so the attempt to 'bridge' these gaps is central to global reform. The Brandt Reports described the mutual interdependence between countries of the 'north' and 'south'. It suggested that, through the dismantling of trade agreements between rich countries, more favourable prices should be paid for Third-World goods to make competition more equitable. In addition, the reports recommended that the international community should finance agricultural research and development in the 'south' rather than exporting arms to them.

 ## 4 Globalisation

The increasing cultural, political and economic relationship between disparate societies is described as globalisation.

- Patterns of sociability have changed.

- Business and politics operate on a global rather than national scale.

Harvey and Giddens describe the inexorable growth of communication networks, which compresses time and space, as the catalyst of a new world order. In addition, Giddens believes that globalisation has two other distinct features. Our patterns of sociability and communication have moved from 'local' or personal relationships to global ones. For example, instead of consulting our friends we consult professional experts for advice and help. People have also become more reflective; identities are not fixed but subjected to reconsideration and readjustment.

For Barraclough (1978), globalisation is economic, or as Riddell claims, 'the real power lies with global business'. Computer technology has allowed goods to be produced on a global scale, which has led to domination of many markets by one company. For instance, the Sony 'Playstation' is genuinely global. In many cases, multinational companies have branches in many countries, and products are comprised of parts built all around the world. Bell describes the presence of inter-governmental agencies such as the UN as an expression of political globalisation. With the omnipresent threat of nuclear and chemical warfare, it has been seen that some issues are just too big or ubiquitous for nations to deal with individually (e.g. the conflict between the Israelis and Palestinians).

However, there has been considerable resistance to handing over sovereignty to organisations like the European Union. Particularly in Britain, there has been a concerted effort to maintain sovereignty. Cultural globalisation implies a synthesis of different lifestyles around the world. There is both a striking similarity in the way people live their lives and interact with the media, and a celebration of different regions and cultures. Today, everything has a global dimension – for instance, Hollywood films are shown around the world and may act as a platform for advertisers to export their goods to foreign markets. For some, this is American cultural imperialism, which generates demand for American products and its way of life.

 ## The role of aid, trade and transnational corporations

Many developing countries experience investment in some form from a number of richer, foreign sources. This section will highlight:

- the benefits of loans, financial aid and transnational corporations operating in developing countries

- the arguments detailing the negative impact of foreign 'investment'.

The consensual opinion on transnational corporations (TNCs) is that they have a negative impact on developing and less-developed countries. In contrast to this prevailing view, Harris applauds the deliberate attempts by governments to aid companies, who in return bring new technology and equipment, forge new markets, import and nurture expertise and help development. However, their presence is also an indication of the continuing inequality of power relationships between the rich 'north' and the impoverished 'south'. Jenkins concludes that the actions of TNCs lead to exploitation of the work force, rapid urban development (and accompanying problems), environmental costs and lack of democracy.

Cities in poorer countries have a push/pull effect on the population. Increasing population and mechanisation in the agricultural sector has pushed people towards the city where, despite poor living conditions, life is likely to be better than in the country. Where multinationals move into poorer countries, wages are suppressed because, amongst other reasons, labour is less organised. Often, the workforce remains unskilled because experts are 'imported'. In addition, the predicament of the unemployed is not improved by economic expansion because it is often capital and machinery intensive.

The environment is compromised by increases in population (for example, the need for intensive farming methods) and it is thought that the balance of nature and technology is lost. Saro-Wiwa's execution by the Nigerian authorities was a result of his campaign to force Shell to pay compensation for alleged environmental damage.

Commercial banks have also made vast amounts of money from the interest earned on loans to poorer nations. Likewise, the actions of the International Monetary Fund (IMF), whose role is to lend money to countries experiencing economic difficulties, are seen as detrimental because their overall effect is recessionary and often exacerbate the situation of the poorest in society. Conditions are always imposed when loans are released, for example imports are often severely reduced, as is expenditure on public services, health, education and the infrastructure. Third-world aid is often tied into the expenditure of most Western liberal-democratic countries or is provided by non-governmental organisations (e.g. Oxfam), which focus on poverty relief. In emergency situations, aid of this type has been hugely beneficial. Right-wing theorists see aid as a problem, because it creates a dependency culture, and is often administered badly or spent on inappropriate items. However, like the loans made by the IMF, aid often has conditions attached, which allows richer countries to dominate others, especially in forging new markets.

 Population

Increase in population is seen as a problem in the Third World. Increases in some parts of the world (for example, Africa, where famine has been rife) are seen to be outstripping resources. In this section, we will review theories that advocate an equal redistribution of income and self-help.

Birth rates do appear to be falling as a result of government policies. Alongside these decreases, infant mortality rates are also falling, and people are living longer. The radical position, articulated by George, argues that hunger and population increases reflect the failure of the political and economic system. In short, poverty has to be eradicated. A more equal distribution of income is associated with a decline in birth rates. For example, in many poor countries, where mortality rates are high and welfare provisions non-existent, people will have many children to ensure that there is somebody to look after them in sickness and old age. An improvement in health provisions would result in a decline in the infant mortality rate, which is associated with a reduction in the fertility rate. Simmons and Tunay argue that the best way to achieve this is to move from hospital-based care to community primary care, where care is provided by local people. Furthermore, countries should be encouraged to produce more food for themselves rather than for export; the problem is not over-population but the production and distribution of goods.

 ## 7 Gender and development around the world

Theorists such as Mies (1986) argue that the social, political, economic and global nature of development has created a female global caste. We will explore the arguments, which suggest that women occupy a secondary role to men, despite development.

Illich describes how the pre-industrial 'regime of gender' resulted in patriarchal domination and cruder exploitation. For example, most aid appears to go to those governments which tend to be authoritarian and suppressive of women in particular. Leghorn and Parker describe the exploitation of women in three ways. In some cultures, women have minimal power, characterised by having little freedom and being subjected to high levels of violence (for example, Ethiopia and Japan). They identify other cultures as 'token', where some freedom is allowed in creating networks (for example, the USA). The third type of culture is one in which women enjoy a negotiating role by having greater access to resources and economic power (for example, China). According to this study, economic and social advancements do not go hand in hand, as suggested by the United Nations World Development Report (1995), which concluded that the lesser developed the economy, the less rights women enjoyed.

45 minutes

Use your knowledge

1 Compare and contrast theories of dependency and modernisation.

2 What do we mean by the term 'globalisation'?

3 How far do you agree with the statement that 'explanations of development tend to reflect the ideological position of the theorist'?

Sociology of Crime and Deviance

25 minutes

Test your knowledge

1 Deviance is a _____ concept. In the past, many activities, both legal and otherwise, have been stigmatised. Therefore, deviance is a _____ _____ – i.e. behaviour is not objectively 'deviant'; somebody somewhere defines it as such. Each situation has its own set of _____ or acceptable forms of behaviour. Sanctions may be _____ (rewards) or _____ (punishment). They can also be _____ or _____.

2 Non-sociological ways of explaining deviance focus on individuals by examining perceived _____ and _____ 'abnormalities'. Sheldon (1956) argued that somebody's _____ was a factor in their criminality. However, research in this area is deeply flawed, because it ignores _____ factors. Eysenck (1970) believed that a criminal mind is largely _____ ; criminals are more _____ than the normal population.

3 The functionalist account, articulated by Durkheim, argued that deviance is functional, _____ and _____. It is functional because it can lead to change. In _____ (1897), Durkheim argued that deviance increases during times of great social change. This is known as _____. Merton (1957) argued that there were five ways of reacting to the pressure of conformity. Most people conform, but others become _____ , _____ , _____ or _____ .

4 The interactionist approach looks at the _____ process. This is primarily associated with the work of _____. Once labelled, people act out the '_____- _____' prophecy. Lemert's (1972) model of deviation distinguishes between _____ and _____ deviation. Cohen's work, _____ _____ _____ _____ _____ , focused on how the media _____ disturbances between 'mods' and 'rockers', creating more trouble later on.

5 Marxists argue that the _____ is a consequence of economic factors, including what we believe to be acceptable or unacceptable modes of behaviour. The _____ _____ are the sole beneficiaries of the rules and regulations. Crimes such as theft are seen as _____ acts against the _____ state. Pearce's (1976) work focuses on the authorities' preoccupation with _____- _____ _____. The neo-Marxist perspective on deviance questions the straightforward relationship between the 'structure' of society and deviance. The thinkers associated with this approach are known as the _____ _____. Lee and Young divide crime and deviance into three broad categories: those who are _____ _____ , '_____- _____' groups, and _____ groups.

6 Gilroy and Hall argue that the _____ policies of the police and the _____ perpetuate the black criminal stereotype. In _____ _____ _____ , Hall argues that economic problems were masked by concentrating on the _____ _____.

7 Women are less likely to be _____ and more likely to _____. Heidensohm and Carlan argue that the male-dominated society controls women more effectively than men. This is known as _____ _____. An example of this is women's fear of violent attack in the _____ _____.

8 Statistics on crime are the most _____ of all officially published figures. According to the _____ _____ Survey, many crimes are not reported or recognised.

Answers

1 relative, social construction, norms, positive, negative, formal, informal
2 physical, psychological, physicality, cultural, inherited, extrovert
3 universal, relative, *Suicide*, anomie, retreatists, ritualists, innovators, rebels
4 labelling, Becker, self-fulfilling, primary, secondary, *Folk Devils and Moral Panics*, amplified 5 superstructure, ruling class, political, capitalist, working class crime, new realists, relatively deprived, 'sub-cultural', marginal
6 racist, media, *Policing the Crisis*, black mugger 7 deviant, conform, control theory, public sphere 8 unreliable, British Crime

✔ If you got them all right, skip to page 85

Sociology of Crime and Deviance

45 minutes

 Improve your knowledge

1 What is deviance?

This section will explore the following:

- that deviance is a relative concept

- defining, sociologically, what we mean by the terms 'deviance', 'crime', 'norms', 'values' and 'sanctions'.

The sociology of deviance (incorporating the sociological study of criminal activity) is *not* the same as criminology, which explicitly focuses on the causes of crime and how to reduce it. Sociology's remit is much broader in scope; its multi-discursive character ensures that 'legal' deviation (social non-conformity rather than illegal activity) is also subjected to the scrutiny of the sociologist. This raises a very important question: What is deviance and what does it mean to be a deviant? Literally, to deviate means to move away from something, but in sociological terms what are people moving away from and how? By broadening the area of study beyond criminology, deviance is not a static but an ever-changing and thus nebulous concept; it changes from place to place, and at different historical moments (re: Foucault's *Crime and Punishment, History of Sexuality* and *Civilisation and Madness*).

Giddens (1997) and Cohen (1977) remind us to consider *whose* rules are actually being broken. Who is defining the deviant act? Students must remember that deviance is a social construction, behaviour is not objectively 'deviant'; somebody somewhere defines it as such, and this changes over time, reflecting the power base (Foucault). So, many different forms of behaviour may be socially condemned or challenged, even if they are not specifically illegal.

Each situation, therefore, has its own set of norms (acceptable forms of behaviour). All social norms are accompanied by sanctions for keeping to or deviating from them, which may be positive (reward) or in the case of non-conformity, negative (punishment). Sanctions are formal or informal. A formal-positive sanction is an official recognition of achievement; for example, receiving certificates for passing exams. This 'norm' is justified because it is

Key points from AS in a Week

Methods and assumptions of the social approach
page 12

Conformity and obedience
pages 12–14

directed towards achieving a particular value – education, which is a precondition for career success – another value. An example of a formal-negative sanction is an official punishment administered by the state when the behaviour of an individual breaks the formal, written rules and regulations known as laws. Laws are norms defined and enforced by the state, which citizens must follow. Depending on the crime, the sanction can take the form of a custodial sentence, community service and/or a fine. An informal-positive sanction could be a nod of approval or smile in reaction to a person's presence or actions, whereas an informal-negative sanction is achieved when somebody intentionally fails to acknowledge a person's presence at a social gathering.

As we have noted, negative sanctions, or more precisely, punishments, can be administered in a variety of ways. It is commonly thought that in liberal democracies, laws reflect the general will of the people. Durkheim describes crime as an act against the people's will and states that punishment serves a necessary function in re-establishing social equity and balance.

However, Foucault observed that a crime committed within the Kingdom was, however trivial, an attack to the King's body and so the criminal's body was attacked in retaliation. In *Crime and Punishment*, Foucault details how the regicide's body is subjected to a lengthy, detailed and meticulously administered torture and execution. This meticulousness of detail was transferred to more 'liberal' forms of punishment. Liberal thinkers argued that in most cases, punishment by death was barbaric, arguing instead that taking somebody's liberty was a fitting, if not worse form of punishment. Prisons, therefore, became a place for discipline, conformity and reform. Prisons are relatively new institutions and, until the 18th century, acted essentially as holding bays for the condemned man or woman. According to Foucault, the more 'liberal' approach was no better or worse than the system of punishment it replaced; ultimately each had the same objective: exercising power and control over people's bodies. This theory can be transposed to contemporary living, where other organisations (schools, hospitals, asylums) emerged, with their own, but very similar rules and regulations and classifying schemes. All impose discipline in a very similar way. As Turner showed, we go on to internalise and act out that discipline and regulation ourselves (self-panopticism). As a consequence, true individuality is suppressed; our ability to express ourselves is regulated and we comply rather than deviate.

2 Non-sociological ways of explaining deviance

The sociology of deviance is concerned with understanding the response of people to society. However, other thinkers focus on individuals by examining perceived physiological and psychological 'abnormalities'.

The earliest explanations of crime and deviance that relate to sociology began to circulate around the turn of the 20th century. Theorists such as Broca and Lombroso argued that deviant or criminal behaviour was biologically determined. By examining the skulls of criminals, Lombrosso identified criminals as having certain 'primitive' physical characteristics including large jaws, acute sight and an exaggerated sex-drive. Similarly, Sheldon (1956) argued that a person's physicality was a factor – muscular people were more likely to engage in criminal activity than thin or fat people.

Research methods that focus on an individual's physicality are highly problematic because they tend to ignore social and environmental factors. If research is focused primarily on prisons and young offenders' homes, it is limited in its scope. As Giddens (1997) points out, judges and court officials may have been more inclined to sentence a 'fleshy' or 'tough' young delinquent to an offenders' home rather than the 'skinny' youth. In addition, male prisoners, living in a macho culture of toughness, with time on their hands and access to a range of training facilities, may be disproportionately more likely to exercise to build up their muscles than the general public. It should be recognised that cultural and environmental as well as physical factors can determine one's physique.

Other researchers offer a psychological explanation. Criminality and deviance is linked with types of personality; a minority of people are described as psychopaths, which accounts for and explains their complete disregard for others people's physical and mental wellbeing. Eysenck (1970) argued that a link existed between criminal behaviour and personality type. He believed that it is largely inherited; criminals inherit a 'criminal' gene. Those who occupy prisons are more extrovert than the normal population, they are less likely to conform and obey rules and more likely to 'live for the moment'.

Sociologists react sceptically to such arguments. First, most studies do not account for social factors. Second, most studies ignore or are not able to study the majority of criminals who are not caught. Third, where do we draw the line between and start connecting psychopathic and criminal traits? For instance, when does a heroic act become an insane one and who defines it as such? As Giddens (1997) argues, it is impossible to disentangle hereditary and environmental factors.

3 Functionalism and deviance

Functionalism is influenced by the analogy of society as a biological organism; when all systems work in conjunction with one another (the heart, lungs, brain, etc.) so does the body. Society is the same: all of its systems must work together for it to function as it should. This section will review how:

- functionalism perceives the 'role' of deviance

- it has influenced sub-cultural theories.

The functionalist account stresses order as a prerequisite to achieving effective social life. Parsons argued that society is divided into four sub-systems: the economy, politics, kinship and community, and cultural organisations. Each is interdependent on one another. Order is achieved by these sub-systems promoting the accepted norms and values. For example, the institutions of the family and school socialise the child with the 'correct' values and patterns of behaviour. Furthermore, there is security derived from belonging to something 'bigger' (the four sub-systems) and this maintains order in everyday life (Shils, 1972).

Durkheim argued that deviance is universal and normal. In every society, some people deviate from the norms. Deviance is relative; what is defined as 'deviant' varies from one cultural group to another. In some countries, adultery is punishable by death, whereas in many countries it carries no legal penalty. In some circumstances, deviance is functional to society, providing it does not reach an excessive proportion. If it does, it then becomes dysfunctional. Society changes, as do its rules. Where governments have mistakenly implemented the 'wrong' policy or been slow to react to public opinion (the collective will), deviant behaviour has initiated or forced changes (for example, the 'poll tax' riots in Britain in the 1980s). On the other hand, deviance stimulates social disapproval from the rest of (law-abiding) society, which in turn reaffirms what constitutes acceptable behaviour. It draws a line between 'them' and 'us' (the conforming majority). This is known as 'boundary maintaining' or 'bonding'. Bonding, or the lack of it, was one of Durkheim's central preoccupations. He was interested in how society was able to maintain itself against growing individualism, arguing that too little bonding created a state of anomie, a feeling of disorientation and not belonging, which would result in increasing social problems.

In his study, *Suicide* (1897) Durkheim argued that deviance increases during times of great social change. When people are left without clear rules or guidelines to live by, they become prone to deviance. Using a comparative method, Durkheim found that rates of suicide could be connected to external social factors. He identified four types of suicide. Egoistic suicides came about from increased individuality and weakened community ties. Altruistic suicides were most common in individuals who belonged to groups whose bonds were *too* strong – people killed themselves for the good of the group (for example, religious cults). Fatalistic suicides were most prominent in societies that were too regulated. Anomic suicides resulted from a lack of social order and regulation by the social group. Durkheim concluded that the higher rate of suicides in some societies could be related to the religious affiliation of the community. Protestants were more likely to commit suicide because their communities did not offer the same collective identity and support as Roman Catholic communities.

One of the problems with Durkheim's study is that it ignores the idea that suicides are a social construction – by relying on coroners' verdicts, it fails to allow that some coroners may have been less likely, for religious reasons, to offer a suicide verdict. Secondly, Durkheim's elucidation serves up a rather interesting dilemma, because the very acknowledgement of crime and deviance suggests that society is not as 'ideal' as he proposes.

Durkheim's work has influenced a plethora of sociologists who have devised their own sub-cultural theories to explain the prevalence of crime and deviance in contemporary society. They tend to argue that:

- society has values that many cannot meet
- reactions to this 'failure' vary, depending on social environment.

Merton (1957) argued that the most resilient value of Western society is the need to do well and acquire material belongings. It assumes that anyone can succeed whatever their starting point in life. However, the likelihood of failure is high for many. Great pressure is still exerted on individuals to do well and if they fail, they are condemned for not succeeding. According to Merton, deviance is a rational response to failure.

So how do people respond to this pressure? Most people conform by accepting the socially-endorsed values and actively pursue success. However, others respond less favourably. Some people become 'innovators', they accept the socially-endorsed values but pursue them through illegal activities. Another deviant response comes from 'ritualists'. Typically, these people will be compulsive, they have no ambition or prospects and they have lost all hope of acquiring the rewards attached to doing well. People who have completely abandoned the competitive outlook and opt for an alternative way of life, choosing to live on the periphery, are described by Merton as 'retreatists'. In contrast, 'rebels' more actively reject existing norms by campaigning for social (and political) change.

Similarly, other sociologists fused anomie with differential association to explain why deviance persisted in certain sub-cultural groups. Cloward and Ohlin (1960) identified lack of opportunity as the main differentiating factor between those who commit crime and those who conform. Their study of delinquent boys found that they endorsed the dominant values (they desired material success) but had very little chance of achieving them because their class position excluded them from pursuing a 'normal' life. The Chicago School, particularly through the work of Sutherland, showed that those living in the 'transition zones' of large cities (areas that had high patterns of migration and lack of community) were more likely to commit crimes. Sutherland argued that in these areas sub-cultural groups encouraged criminal activities in order to pursue the same aims as those working in 'normal' jobs. However, other sub-cultural theorists such as Cohen (1955) have argued that gangs involved in crime were essentially rejecting society's values and creating 'oppositional' values instead. Likewise, Miller (1962), regarded lower-class delinquency as a distinctive culture. He argued that working-class life is characterised by certain 'focal concerns' – a liking for toughness and masculinity.

The interactionist approach differs significantly from structural accounts because it does not look at the act of deviance itself. Instead this approach chooses to study:

- the labelling process – the social construction of 'deviancy'

- the subsequent interaction between the labelled person and the rest of society.

For Becker, 'the central fact about deviance' is that 'it is created by society'. It is not until the act or individual is labelled as deviant that the person becomes deviant. In other words, 'deviance is not a quality of the act the person commits, but rather the consequence of the application by others of the rules and sanctions to an offender'. No action is inherently 'criminal', it depends on how society responds to different situations and different contexts. Deviance is not about what you do but how others perceive and respond to you and your actions. According to Becker, if you are labelled as a deviant, not only is it hard to 'shake off' but the label, 'delinquent', 'deviant' and 'criminal' can become an all-encompassing, evaluating term. However, as with the Tony Martin case (the Norfolk farmer who shot a young intruder), the process of labelling in many cases is not clear cut, nor are the responses by the labelled person and the public as a whole.

The self-fulfilling prophecy is of central importance to the interactionist study of deviance. Becker identifies a process of labelling and subsequent rejection from social groupings. This, in turn, leads to amplification – for example, employers dismiss the deviant. Without a job, the person starts on a downward spiral, which leads to other (perhaps related) criminal activity, resulting in imprisonment. Prison offers the deviant access to fellow deviants, who offer a support community and network. The individual is likely to become completely immersed in the deviant lifestyle, allowing them to justify their actions with like-minded deviants. The individual now assumes the label.

Lemert's (1972) model of deviation bears similarities with Becker's. Lemert distinguishes between primary and secondary deviation. Primary deviation is how the act or crime is treated initially. For an act to move from primary deviation to the secondary stage depends upon a number of different factors, for example, the individual's ability to negotiate with the authorities, their gender, ethnicity, class position and those attributes (or labels) commonly associated with them. Circourel showed in his work, *The Social Justice of Juvenile Justice* (1977), that class position, ethnicity, age and 'potential' for criminality is more likely to move somebody to a secondary stage (i.e. being convicted of a criminal act) and the stimulus to 'learning to be deviant' has begun.

In his work, *Asylums* (1968), Goffman studied people in psychiatric hospitals and argued that once they are institutionalised, an individual's self-identity is removed. This process, which is described as 'mortification', serves only to confirm rather than rehabilitate the person's deviance. Once released, the individual carries the stigma of mental illness for the rest of their lives – they were once a mental patient.

One of the most famous studies on labelling theory and deviance amplification was Cohen's *Folk Devils and Moral Panics*. He showed how excessive and blatant misreporting by the media provoked interest in what was in fact no more than a minor disturbance between a few youths. However, public reaction and continued media exposure created a spiral of amplification in which the 'mods' and 'rockers' were portrayed as *folk devils* (threatening the moral boundaries of acceptability). The subsequent events could be described as a classic self-fulfilling prophecy – the dramatic publicity about expected confrontations attracted many more young people to particular 'hot-spots' where fighting took place. Inadvertently, the media helped to create the events it deplored.

One of the major criticisms levelled at labelling theory, is that it appears to be deterministic – if a person is labelled 'bad', they become 'bad'. However, Young's study on hippie culture in Notting Hill shows that if the would-be hippie is to enjoy the effects of marijuana, they have to *learn* how to smoke the drug properly. Similarly, those people convicted of criminal behaviour are exposed to increased interaction with criminals and criminal opportunity. Anecdotal evidence suggests that prison does not reform but teaches criminals better methods.

Labelling theory does not offer an explanation for the origins of primary deviance. Why do certain men and women behave in the way they do? Cornish and Clarke (1986) and Feeney (1986) criticise interactionism for concentrating on reaction rather than action. In many ways, criminals are like shoppers – they are rational and their decision to commit crime rests on the situation they find themselves in.

5 The Marxist perspective

Marxists argue that if society is to function efficiently, social order is necessary. However, the way in which capitalist society is organised determines the nature of law and order and thus crime and deviance. They argue that:

- the superstructure is a consequence of economic factors, including what we believe to be acceptable and unacceptable modes of behaviour
- the ruling class are the sole beneficiaries of the rules and regulations.

Marxists argue that the ruling class gain far more from the smooth running of society than the other classes. Althusser proposed that they maintain and impose a social order by a variety of means through different ideological (family, school, media and religion) and repressive (courts, police and army) state agencies, which play a crucial part in promoting conformity and order against the *real* interests of the working class. The ruling class have the power to define what is acceptable and the neutrality of the law is a facade; laws work in favour of a narrow set of interests. For example, Hirst describes dominant ideology as bourgeois ideology. Labour is another word for 'exploitation', because workers do not receive their true 'market' price for work that has little intrinsic value. Capitalists extract the surplus value and laws uphold this as 'fair'.

Marxists argue that crime is an inevitable feature of capitalist society because such a society promotes greed and self-interest; it is an aggressive and competitive ideology with few winners and many losers. Moreover, the system perpetuates injustice and so the working class revert to crime, which challenges the dominant ideas and social order (re: Abercrombie and Turner and Gilroy). An individual theft may also be viewed as an overtly political act; as a statement of non-compliance. Instead of trying to purchase possessions, why not take them? On the other hand, if the act of theft was not intentionally political, it still has profound consequences for a system that is reliant on the exchange of goods, hence the need for government agencies to 'manage' particular sorts of crime (for example, advertising campaigns to dissuade people from purchasing 'pirate' videos). Also, crime can relate to objective material conditions. For example, people will resort to stealing if they are poor and hungry.

In Pearce's (1976) *Crimes of the Powerful* he describes law and order as an ideological tool of the ruling class, intended to make sure that the working class conform, hence the obsessive public moral concern with lower-class crime. According to Pearce, the money, time and energy spent on controlling it (and reporting it) diverts attention from the exploitative activities of the capitalist class. The real criminals are those who enforce it, because other crime is ignored or seen as 'legitimate' (for example, tax evasion). Pearce's evaluation is supported by many unrelated studies, including American government reports, which estimate that business fraud and 'white-collar' crime dwarf the amount of 'ordinary' crime. In Britain, it is estimated that middle-class crime costs ten times more than social security crime, yet government campaigns and political agendas are preoccupied with 'smashing' benefit fraud. Business fraud and 'white-collar' crimes are hard, sometimes impossible, to detect and very rarely do they come to the public's attention as a consequence.

From the neo-Marxist perspective, in Taylor, Walton and Young's *The New Criminology*, it is argued that crime 'grows' from inequalities in wealth and power. However, to them, Marx was too economically deterministic in his theory, wrongly assuming that external forces direct the activities of criminals. Taylor *et al* prefer to argue that individuals often choose to break the law and so crime should be understood in a more 'holistic' way:

- First, it is important to understand the way wealth and power are distributed in society.

- Second, the circumstances and context of the individual act have to be considered.

- Third, why did the deviant act take place? What meaning did it have for those responsible? Was it a political act?

- Fourth, how did other people react to the act of deviance? How did it affect the victim?

- Fifth, how was the act treated by the powerful in society? Does the reaction differ to other deviant acts/different actors?

- Sixth, labelling theory should be utilised. How do people respond to their label? Do they accept or reject the label?

It is argued that by combining the above elements, the sociologist can present a 'complete' theory of crime and deviance.

Sociology of Crime and Deviance

The new-left-realist group, Young, Lea, Matthews and Kinsey, attack the 'blinkered' approach of Marxist-influenced sociological study. Increased crime rates are real and not statistical abnormalities or racist fabrications. In particular, the left-realists attack neo-Marxist and Marxist criminologists for denying that some crimes are more common among ethnic minorities. Of course, they accept that a number of factors can exaggerate the black crime rate: poor housing, economic and social isolation, unemployment, policing policies and 'institutional' racism (re: the Stephen Lawrence case and subsequent McPherson Report). They also tackle the Marxist 'idealists' for their romanticism and politicisation of crime, ignoring that the working class are also more likely to be its victims. Instead, the new-left-realists claim to have redressed the whole issue of crime by taking a more considered approach, looking at all types of crime seriously, offering descriptions as well as prescriptions.

According to Lee and Young, crime and deviance can be separated into three broad categories. In prosperous societies, when people compare themselves to others they can feel relatively deprived. As society grows richer, accompanied by higher standards of living, expectations rise too; what are luxuries today are necessities tomorrow. However, there will always be restricted opportunities of achieving success for many groups and this will act as a catalyst to commit crime. Some sub-cultural groups that share the conditions of relative deprivation develop lifestyles to cope with their economic predicament. Other groups who lack a political and economic organisation to represent their interests can be described as marginal groups. These groups – for example, the unemployed – may suffer from resentment and the problems that accompany an unrewarding and unfulfilling life. With no body or group to represent them and forward their interests, they are pushed further towards the periphery of society, and are more prone to turn to crime, violence and other forms of deviance.

Lee and Young's analysis raises a number of questions, the most significant being: what is to be done about law and order? In response, Kinsey, Young and Lee made several suggestions to improve policing practices. Confidence in the police is low for many reasons. Clear-up rates are low, time spent on investigations is low and the police are seen by some as the 'enemy'. They propose that an accountable, democratic police authority should be installed, where the public has a direct say on policies and guidelines. In addition, they also offer 'macro' solutions, that is, tackling the social causes of crime by ensuring greater equality, opportunity and freedom of choice within society. This may include well-planned housing (i.e. not havens for muggers), greater leisure facilities, and reducing income inequality by reducing unemployment and creating jobs with 'real' prospects. Unfortunately, in the final analysis, they do not detail how all of these solutions should be addressed.

 ### 6 Ethnicity and crime

It was noted in the previous section that statistics on crime show that a disproportionate number of young black men commit crime. In this section we will be looking at the views of two theorists, Gilroy and Hall, who argue that:

- racist policies of the police create a myth of black criminality

- the media helps to perpetuate the black criminal stereotype.

Gilroy asserts that crimes by some minority groups are deliberate political acts, in the sense that these groups are actively defending themselves and 'hitting back' at society, which treats black and Asian people unjustly. He argues that 'the scars of imperialist violence' act as the catalyst for people to resist their exploitation, police harassment, racially motivated attacks and discrimination (hence the 'riots' of the 1980's). The police force, which is predominantly white, holds racist views about particular groups of people. This impacts on crime statistics. Therefore, the figures cannot be trusted. They are more likely to arrest members of these communities regardless of whether they have committed a crime or not.

Gilroy argues that economic crises label the immigrant community as employment surplus and this fuels the myth of criminality and the argument for repatriation often resurfaces. In *Policing the Crisis*, Hall argues that economic problems produce social crises; the context of the problems faced by British capitalism in the early 1970s was characterised by rising unemployment and inflation (stagflation) coupled with falling wages. These problems undermined what Hall describes as a 'class-truce', or a period of hegemonic stability, which existed from 1945 to the early 1970's. Hall's study was concerned with the social reaction to crime and the distribution of power as a whole.

The 'crisis of capitalism' was accompanied by a 'new' crime, called 'mugging', which was associated with the 'influx' of black immigrants. However, in reality it was not a new crime, just a 'new' name for street robbery. The economic crisis provided a fertile environment for increasing crime rates, but it was the press who were responsible for orchestrating public opinion and directing attention and anger against the 'black mugger', who became symbolic of the immigrant threat. Hall describes this response as a (distorted) media 'moral panic', which masked the real problem. Capitalism was in crisis, but society's impression of and exposure to events were fuelled by the media's reaction to immigration, blaming 'outsiders' for threatening the stability of society instead of accepting that the capitalist system was collapsing under its own inherent contradictions.

The police set up 'special' sections to deal with this tide of crime, often resorting to forceful methods. Hall suggests that the police actually amplified the deviance they were supposed to control, through increased harassment of young black males.

Downes and Rock argued that Hall's study was contradictory. On one hand, it claimed that the increase in black crime was due to labelling, whilst on the other, it 'admitted' that black criminal activity increased due to the pressures of unemployment. Does this imply the threat was as 'real' as the media portrayed it? Young argued that the public should have been worried about 'muggings' or any other serious street crime because the frequency of these crimes had been increasing. He also argued that the study did not provide evidence that the public, as opposed to the media, were panicking about mugging, nor did it show that the public identified 'mugging' with black men.

 Gender and crime

According to Smart (1977), the sociology of crime and deviance reflects the 'male-centric' nature of sociology in general. Although men commit most crimes, Heidensohn believes that there is a common misconception about female criminology; it lacks the 'glamour' of male criminology, because it tends to focus on inconsequential crimes such as shoplifting. This section seeks to explain:

- why women are less likely to be deviant and more likely to conform

- the impact of 'women's liberation' on female criminal activity.

Earlier 'social' theorists and criminologists such as Lombroso argued that the biological makeup of women prevented them from being criminal. According to Pollak (1950), there were two reasons why women appeared less in crime statistics. First, biologically, women were naturally adept at hiding crime – for example, social taboos have forced women to hide menstrual pain. Second, policemen (males) acted in a 'chivalrous' way towards women and action would not be pursued. Sociologically, there is very little evidence to support both theorists' views; they can be accused of perpetuating unsubstantiated stereotypical images of women. Can we accept that women are naturally less likely to commit crime?

According to Home Office figures, women only make up approximately 3.5% of those convicted of violent crime. Heidensohn and Carlan put forward control theory – male-dominated society controls women more effectively than it does men. Sex/gender roles and social arrangements restrict and limit opportunities for criminality. Box and Heidensohn both recognised that women's opportunity to commit crime was limited because a woman's place was seen to be in the home (private sphere). Socialisation and parents' perceptions of what constitutes 'proper' female behaviour play a very important role; girls are 'protected' against deviance by being denied the same freedoms as their brothers, developing a 'bedroom culture' (Smart) instead of one that is public.

Women's fear of violent attack (sexual assault, rape) limits women's participation in the public sphere. Brownmiller claims that rape and the fear of rape 'is nothing more or less than a conscious process of intimidation by which all men keep all women in a state of fear'. Feminist theorists argue that when many women challenge patriarchal values they are forced into conformity through domestic violence.

Box regards the leniency debate as lacking understanding because women who commit serious crimes are dealt with in the same manner as their male counterparts. Similarly, Farrington and Morris (1979) showed that discrepancies in sentencing disappeared when the severity of the crime was taken into account. However, there are several theorists who argue that the system is biased against women, especially in rape trials, where men are often dealt with more sympathetically and domestic violence treated more leniently. Heidensohn and Allen argue that the law is based on traditional definitions of gender: women are believed to be more central to the family, so stereotypical notions mean that women are less likely to be sent to prison.

The only crime where there seems to be some convergence between males and females is shoplifting. Where the opportunity to commit crime in a public sphere is more or less equal, then the likelihood of both sexes committing a crime is more equal. An experiment using 'lost letters' by Farrington and Kidd (1980) found that women were as likely as men to steal if the opportunity presented itself. Also, studies by Campbell (girl gangs in New York, 1986) and Carlen (Holloway Prison, 1985) cast doubt over the argument that crime is the domain of the male.

Alder (1975) argued that women's liberation had led to a new type of female criminal. For example, women committing robberies had increased at a much faster rate than men. It would seem to follow that as society becomes more egalitarian, social roles in both legitimate and criminal areas of life should be comparable. This implies that women's liberation is a bad thing and fuels the debate on whether women should stick to their traditional roles.

The premise of Carlen's study of female prisoners is that humans are rational and they will turn to crime when the advantages outweigh the disadvantages. Carlen concluded that women turn to crime when class and gender 'deals' are not met. In other words, when women do not experience any intrinsic satisfaction, do not receive the wages and material rewards from their work or are not fulfilled within the family (i.e. it is too oppressive/abusive), criminality becomes a possibility.

 ## Statistics

Statistics show that crime is rising, but figures about crime are the most unreliable of all officially published figures on social issues. This section will concentrate on the following assertions:

- Britain has become more 'criminal'.

- Crime statistics do not reflect the real rate of crime.

According to official statistics, crime has risen; the 1980s witnessed a doubling of the incidence of crime. In 1996 (*Social Trends*, 1998), 5 million offences were recorded by the police. It is estimated that over half of crimes are not reported.

Official figures are just the tip of a very large iceberg. Reiner (1996) argues that the increases are *real* because people own more property to steal.

Official statistics only show crimes recorded by the police. According to the British Crime Survey (the official estimate of unrecorded crime known to the victim), many crimes are not reported or recognised, and some people are unwilling or unable to report them. Many people live in fear of reprisals and others do not have faith in the police (only 3% of all offences end in a caution or conviction). Others may be too embarrassed to report a crime (e.g. sexual assault). Some people will see certain crime as too trivial to report. It has been suggested that people with insurance cover are more likely to report crimes. However, too much reporting in an area can also make certain postcode districts uninsurable, so this may dissuade people from reporting less serious crimes (Reiner). Self-report studies also suggest much higher rates of crime, but they too are highly problematic, as people often lie. In addition, the way different police forces deal with crime varies from area to area. Some are more efficient than others in their recording of crime, whilst others may manipulate the figures to 'improve' their arrest records. Ironically, police forces that focus on a crime 'problem' usually increase criminality statistics by recording a greater number of convictions. This is known as deviance amplification.

Was there really less crime in the past? As we have noted, factors such as new policing methods and increases in the number of households with insurance may affect crime statistics. However, moral panics point to a fear that violence, in particular, has worsened. As Hall shows in his study on mugging, there is nothing new about street crime. Do increases in crime statistics prove an increase in crime or merely a better awareness and higher levels of reporting? For example, the 'prevalence' of child abuse today would suggest that it is a new phenomenon, but this increase could be due to a change in attitudes, which means that child abuse is more likely to be reported rather than hidden. Caution should be exercised when it appears that a particular crime rate is on the increase.

Sociology of Crime and Deviance

50 minutes

Use your knowledge

1 Why do sociologists react sceptically to 'individualist' explanations of crime and deviance?

2 Compare and contrast interactionist and Marxist accounts of crime and deviance.

3 Why are men more likely to commit crime than women?

4 How has Durkheim's work afforded us a better understanding of crime and deviance?

30 minutes

1 In the 1997 election, Labour targeted 'Mondeo man'. Labour figured that if they could secure his vote, they would win the General Election. In 2001, Conservative Party workers are pursuing 'pebble-dash' people (those who live in semi-detached houses) and hoping to secure their vote for the impending General Election. Both parties will spend millions on their election campaign, hoping to convince the electorate that they are the best party to govern in the 21st century.

(a) Briefly outline the ideological differences between the Labour and Conservative parties. (8 marks)

(b) What does this statement above tell you about the nature of voting in Great Britain today? (12 marks)

2 Underdeveloped countries are the helpless victims of the brutal capitalist world. Some sociologists liken it to a street beggar who holds their hand out for assistance only to receive the odd penny or two for a 'cup of coffee'. Like the street beggar, the underdeveloped country is most likely to suffer illness, abuse and assault. There is always somebody to 'help out', but you have to do them a 'favour' in return – the knight in shining armour happens to be the dark prince. From then on things become much worse; a spiral of exploitation ensues. Back on the street, the beggar asks for a few pence but they are told by the rich passers-by to 'get a job' and sort themselves out.

(a) What kind of explanation of development is being described above? (1 mark)

(b) How do countries move from an underdeveloped stage to a developed one? (9 marks)

(c) Do transnational companies aid or hinder development? (10 marks)

The underclass is a dangerous and nasty section of society. It is a 'cancer' that feeds off the labour of decent hard-working, law-abiding citizens. They happily live in squalor, even though society has become more prosperous. Instead of working, they skive; working is an alien concept. They have abandoned all dignity and self-respect, they ask the state, cap-in-hand, for handouts, which are invariably spent on cigarettes, alcohol and drugs. Furthermore, they continue to have babies even though there are no fathers present. The children, however, still inherit their father's inability to work, observe rules or take responsibility for their actions.

(a) Label the theory described above. (1 mark)
(b) Which thinkers are commonly associated with this approach? (2 marks)
(c) Account for other theories that deal with the concept of the underclass. (7 marks)
(d) Has the gap between the underclass and the rest of society come about due to the convergence between the working and middle class? (10 marks)

 According to the neo-Marxists or new left realists, police racism alone cannot account entirely for the fact that, proportionately, young Afro-Caribbean men are more likely to appear in official crime statistics. Gilroy, in particular, is attacked for overlooking the fact that many crimes committed by black people are on other black people – critics ask how this can be a political attack on the white state. However, in the 'post-Lawrence' era, Gilroy's work gains resonance once more. It has been reported that police officers have complained of being 'shackled' when policing certain districts in fear that they will be accused of being 'racist'. It has been suggested that arrests and crime detection have been detrimentally affected as a consequence. This raises questions regarding the racially motivated nature of policing and about crime committed by certain groups.

(a) Gilroy's work suggests that the official statistics on crime cannot be accurate because of racist policing. What are the other problems regarding official statistics on crime? (6 marks)
(b) How useful is functionalism in presenting an understanding of why crime and deviance takes place? (7 marks)
(c) How important is it to understand the social and biological characteristics of criminality? (7 marks)

Use your Knowledge Answers

Stratification – Inequality and Difference

1 It would seem that with the apparent growth of the middle class, the proposition that mobility has increased since 1944 appears to be strong. For example, Lipset and Bendix and Payne found considerable upward movement from blue-collar to white-collar work. The service class had increased, which meant that it recruited from elsewhere (i.e. the working class), thus upward mobility was occurring. However, mobility and a growing middle class is not the same thing (re: Nuffield study). The studies conducted by Glass (1949), Blau and Duncan found that long-range mobility is rare. It is not relative mobility that has occurred but absolute mobility. The likelihood is that if you are born into a middle-class family you are likely to remain middle class in later life. For example, middle-class families enjoy material and cultural advantages over their working-class counterparts. They have what Bourdieu describes as 'cultural capital'.

2 The functionalists, namely Davis and Moore, stress the 'functional necessity' of stratification in modern societies. Stratification takes place in all capitalist societies and rewards the most productive or important people. This is often linked with the income people receive.

Marxists also believe that class is a fact of capitalism. There are two classes, and to survive, the working class must sell their labour to the bourgeoisie who own the means of production and protect their interests forcefully and ideologically. They too experience differences in income, derived from the ownership and non-ownership of the means of production. Although some Marxists recognise an 'intermediate' class (or contradictory class), the difference between middle class and working class is not as real as their different objective financial situation. If people do not own the means of production they are, by definition, working class. Braverman clearly believes, however, that the 'proletarianisation' of the workplace (especially the middle class) and commensurate decreases in income set against the increasing wealth and power of the ruling class will only serve to strengthen a working-class consciousness.

Weber did argue that ownership of wealth/property is the basis of the class system, but he also argued that stratification has other dimensions. Class may be derived from economic means, but according to Weber, status rather than class forms the basis of commonality and collective action; in other words this is not dependent on income. Likewise, party does not always reflect economic interests.

3 Saunders does not believe that an all-embracing, all-powerful 'ruling class' exists. He describes it as 'an influential economic elite'. Dahrendorf argues similarly that upper-class decomposition has taken place and the control/day-to-day running of companies is by managers rather than owners. Others, namely the Marxists, reject the concept of the 'managerial revolution' but argue that the upper class can be seen as a group, whatever their ownership status, enjoying a 'constellation of interests' (Scott). Miliband and Giddens identify a unified capitalist upper class, which has a distinct educational and cultural background.

Stratification – Sex and Gender

1 The biological accounts argue that the differences between men and women are natural. Sociobiologists rely upon either evolutionary accounts or argue that behaviour is governed by genetic structures. It can also be linked with hormonal differences. Despite cultural changes, men and women still remain different. The functionalist account stresses the biological differences between men and women as well. For example, women are supposed to be naturally predisposed to provide the family warmth, security and emotional support.

Inevitably, the biological accounts are challenged by sociologists. Using a Marxist perspective, inequalities are based on historical conditions. In other words, the dominance of men over women is ideological, it is culturally constructed and maintained. It appears to be natural. Oakley, echoing the work of de Beauvoir, argues that there is no correlation between sex and gender; one is not born but rather becomes a woman. These roles are learnt through the socialisation process; children are bought the 'correct' (or 'gendered') toys and brought up differently. They learn society's expectations, which are presented as natural and true.

2 Feminist sociology describes the unequal distribution of wealth and opportunity between men and women. Sex is the most profound example of a stratification system. Women are described as being subordinate, oppressed and exploited (Engels). Some feminists such as Firestone argue that men are naturally physically superior because they do not have childbearing roles, which limit life chances for women.

In work, women experience poorer working conditions; they tend to be the most expendable and employed in lower status jobs. There are still discrepancies between male and female earners at all levels. This relegates women to the status of a reserve army of labour. Even with 'new' work opportunities, women are more likely to be peripheral workers. Women are also less organised/unionised than men and thus less powerful.

The functionalist account argues that women occupy lower status jobs because they are more likely to have breaks for motherhood. As a result they lag behind male employees by missing out on training opportunities.

Stratification – Ethnicity and Race

1 Earlier theorists were preoccupied with devising biological labels and hierarchies. They believed that different 'races' had very different physical characteristics, which could be linked with their behaviour. For example, media attention has focused on the physical/athletic superiority of black athletes over white athletes. Racism is based on those supposed differences.

However, Jones shows that the number of gene differences between people of the same colour, living in a relatively small region, are very similar to the differences between white and black people. The evidence for 'natural' differences is not very strong, but nevertheless still prevalent today.

People can be divided by ethnicity, which is often more dependent on cultural factors rather than biological factors. Different ways of life are learnt not biologically inherited.

2 Ethnicity appears to be a stratification system in itself. Ethnic minority people tend to occupy the lowest paid jobs, because they tend to be less educated. As the Swann Report showed, racism was endemic in schools, and the impact on young ethnic minority children must be disastrous. Also, because of their lowly class position (and very little economic and 'cultural capital') and their lack of fluency in the elaborated code (Bernstein), their predicament is worsened.

However, the work of Cross and the Ballards sheds light on how the cultural disposition of an individual can determine their life chances. Both argue that many Asian groups are culturally predisposed to be entrepreneurs and so are likely to succeed economically. However, the self-reliance and business orientation of many groups of people could also be the reaction to the racism and prejudice found in the workplace (for example, a response to being laid-off first during bouts of redundancy).

3 Politically, control over immigration is a highly emotive issue. Ever since the 1948 British Nationality Act, governments have sought to control the influx of certain groups of people, usually dark-skinned or poor people. It is believed that that they have entered the country to claim 'generous' welfare benefits, such as income support, housing and free medical treatment.

For functionalists, immigration itself is not a problem. However, it becomes one, when the immigrants fail to comply with the host country's laws and customs. Immigrants, therefore, must assimilate themselves into the country's cultural life. This is very similar to the New Right's criticism of some groups of people residing in the UK today, arguing that some do not and will not comply with the 'British' way of life.

Marxists believe that immigration is an inevitable feature of colonialism and capitalism. Inequalities in development and exploitation have forced people to move and find work in more affluent countries. As a reserve army of labour, the wages of the ethnic minorities are suppressed, which causes hostilities within the working class, which results in division and racism.

Welfare and Poverty

1 New Right or individualistic theories place emphasis on the individual rather than structural factors; poverty is blamed on the behaviour and culture of the poor. The work of Hayek, Saunders, Marsland and Murray have all alluded to the same thing: state intervention is bad, it discourages individualism and independence. Murray describes a culture of dependency that 'traps' people in their predicament rather than helps them – living standards have improved for all groups, yet they lack the individual qualities and 'moral fibre' to take responsibility for their actions.

The Conservative government adopted right-wing policies and a free-market philosophy on welfare and state provisions. Comments by the former Conservative minister, Norman Tebbitt, epitomised his party's response to the unemployed, ordering them to 'get on their bikes' and look for work, in other words, take responsibility.

In evaluation, structural accounts, for example, Marxist and Social Democratic approaches, identify that poverty is a real objective fact and not always the fault of the individual. Marxism, obviously, will always be virulent towards capitalism, arguing that poverty is a natural and inevitable feature. Similarly, social-democratic approaches recognise that the market is not a good provider of welfare provisions, and without intervention, full citizenship cannot be enjoyed, whereas incidences of poverty and its associated problems will be exacerbated.

2 The aim of the Beveridge Report was to eradicate the five giants of poverty: idleness, squalor, want, disease and ignorance. Even though the welfare state was introduced to act as safety net, for many it has done nothing to close the gap between classes. Writers such as Le Grand (1982) showed how the middle class benefited most from state provisions, such as health, education, public transport and social services. The obvious gain has been in education, because it is the middle class who have benefited most from its expansion. For example, they already have the correct 'cultural capital' (Bourdieu) to succeed. Middle-class children do much better than working-class children, even if they have the same IQ (re: Bowles and Gintis). In addition, the public sector is one of the largest employers of middle-class people.

The redistribution of income should, in principle, take from the rich and give to the poor. However, the burden of taxation has been shifted from the upper and middle class to the working class. VAT is a regressive tax. A greater proportion of the poorer household's income is spent on everyday household items and food, therefore they are paying a disproportionate amount of tax. Changes in the economy have resulted in hundreds of thousands of job losses. Unemployed people are, by definition, poor.

Studies have also shown that, despite the introduction of the welfare state, poverty has not been eradicated. Numerous studies have shown that relative poverty in Britain has worsened. According to Townsend and Mack and Lansley, the number of people living in poverty exceeds 10 million people (over one sixth of the population). The New Right describe this situation as inequality, whereas Marxists insist that the lot of the working class and the poor cannot really be improved by capitalism.

3 There are two ways to measure poverty: there is absolute and relative poverty, and their advantages and disadvantages should be discussed. Using the former definition, it can be claimed that Britain has eradicated poverty. A poverty line in the UK has never been officially recognised. It was generally thought that those living below 140% of the supplementary benefit level were poor. One of the first studies conducted by Rowntree was based on the definition of absolute poverty. However, the sociologists Townsend, Mack and Lansley have argued that poverty can only be measured in relation to the accepted living standards of the population.

The Breadline Britain study by Mack and Lansley used a relative definition. Their study allowed the respondents to devise a list or consensual view of what people considered to be an acceptable standard of living. For example, many people did not have access to the most basic necessities.

The criticisms levelled at Townsend *et al*, is that their criteria are too arbitrary. They assume that people behave identically or desire the same things. It is best to see poverty as involuntary.

4 There has been a move to 'privatise' or off-load the services offered by the welfare state onto private organisations such as charities and voluntary bodies. In many sectors 'quangos' have replaced regulatory public bodies (think of Ofsted).

By focusing on education and the health service, students should be aware that both have been 'encouraged' to adopt a more 'business-like' approach. For example, introducing league tables, encouraging competition, managing budgets and operating an internal market. However, to privatise education and the NHS would be political suicide, because there is a general agreement that the market or voluntary organisations cannot provide adequate health and education provisions for all. Certainly, care in the community initiatives for the elderly and the mentally ill have their merits – de-institutionalisation is a good thing – but on the other hand high standards of surveillance and care cannot be guaranteed. Furthermore, for many critics, the care in the community programme is an euphemism for 'homelessness'.

'Private' provisions will run alongside public ones, as we can see with the growth of private pensions. With a growing elderly population, it is considered

that the state can no longer afford to pay its elderly population. In addition, better-off people will opt for private health and pay for education. However, not everyone can afford it, which would worsen social problems further. For Hutton there is no need to resort to private measures, if governments move to longer-term strategies of investment in public provisions rather than looking to the short-term solutions.

Power and Politics

1 The pluralist account, as opposed to Marxism, believes that power can be separated. In general, democracy 'works' by virtue that, in between elections, pressure groups serve to make the government of the day more responsive to economic, political and social events. There is a 'plurality' of groups whose aims are very different; they compete to be heard and to influence policy. It would seem that this model is a fair reflection of politics in Britain today. In addition, the state is neutral, acting as a mediator for different interests. Likewise, the functionalist account believes that power often shifts from the government to people and back again. Power is trust and when trust diminishes, people have the power to vote those in government out.

However, this model is contested by Marxists, who argue that power is finite and that pressure groups, by seeking concessions, help to perpetuate the myth that capitalism is democratic. Power does not shift, it stays rooted in the hands of the ruling class (re: Miliband). The state is a tool of class oppression. Marxists also question how effective pressure groups really are, especially those which do not have access to influential people or funds in order to be heard. Lukes shows how power can be exercised at three different levels, which suggests groups who do not have the power to dictate the agenda lack power.

2 The media is very important; political parties spend millions on election campaigns and media training as it is the dominant way to get the message across. It would seem that the media is in a very powerful position. Depending on which approach the sociologist adopts, the impact of the media will either be great or negligible. 'Old' theories of the media's power to influence the way people think suggest that newspapers or the television can influence the way people vote (e.g. 'It was the *Sun* that won it.'). Katz and Lasersfeld's work (even Hall and Morley's – see the chapter on the Media in *AS Sociology in a Week*) shows that the media's impact may not be as great as it first seemed.

However, the media's influence cannot, on its own, account for how people vote. So students must consider other factors that impact on voting behaviour, for example a person's class position or their upbringing. A full discussion would include an appraisal of the competing viewpoints regarding how and why people vote the way they do.

3 The new right's impact on the landscape of British politics in the 1980's and 1990's was profound. For example, New Labour's 'diluted' socialism, for many critics, is a response to the adoption of free-market policies and the rejection of the post-war consensus. The Labour government has had to work with what they have inherited. For example, due to the privatisation (and subsequent success of the former public utilities) Clause 4 was scrapped (i.e. the commitment to nationalise), they have inherited 'light-touch' regulation, left by the Conservatives, and maintained school league tables.

If a new consensus has been found, it is one that is based upon economic and political freedom; there is a willingness by governments to work alongside businesses to complete 'public' projects, for example the Millennium Dome. In addition, more people hold shares and own their homes. Trades unions' power is very weak. There has been a hardening of policy towards benefit claimants, the rich appear to have become richer, whilst the poor have remained poor. Similarly, care in the community initiatives have placed an extra burden on families and contributed to the homelessness problem.

World Sociology

1 Answers should consider the following:

- Modernisation is comprised of Rostow's economic and technical model.
- Those who argue that culture has to be modernised (i.e. Westernised) (Kerr, McClelland and Hoselitz).
- Similarly, convergence theorists such as Dahrendorf and Bell believe that the world is becoming homogenised.

Modernisation theory can be accused of ethnocentricity, by downplaying the importance of traditional cultures, believing them to be inferior.

From a 'dependency' point of view, inequality takes place on a global scale.

- The structure of undeveloped countries has been created by the exploitative pursuits of capitalist countries.
- Dependency theory, articulated primarily by Frank, describes the drive towards development as inevitably resulting in domination and exploitation by the West.
- 'Real' development cannot take place and a cycle of exploitation takes place: richer, Western countries enjoying beneficial terms of trade by 'creating' market prices and levels.
- Many countries cannot grow independently; their colonial 'masters' ensured that they became dependent on one or two industries. Many countries' infrastructure is also inadequate to deal with any growth.
- Schuurman argues that countries cannot opt out of the capitalist world, or more specifically from a dependency role, because they cannot be self-sufficient.

The similarities between the two can be described thus: Warren concludes that the development of nations provides the correct industrial environment from which a revolutionary conscience will rise. As with modernisation theory, it is believed that the changing structure of society will change the fabric of society.

Use your Knowledge Answers

2
- Countries have become increasingly dependent on one another, which has changed the nature of how people socialise and conduct business (Barraclough).
- This has been facilitated by new computer technology (re: Harvey and Giddens).
- Markets and goods are produced on a global scale, which has led to domination of many markets by one company (e.g. Microsoft). Multinational companies have branches in many countries and politics has moved onto a world platform.

3 Students should show an awareness of:
- Sociology's multi-discursive nature; different viewpoints lead to different interpretations – it relies on the fundamental basics of sociological thought.
- Different ideological positions have different definitions of development.
- Marxism is also a political doctrine; capitalist development will always be seen negatively because it is exploitative; it only works in the interests of the ruling class (re: Frank's 'exploitative spiral').
- New Right or free-market approaches (re: Friedman and Baur) oppose central planning, which cannot provide goods and services. They assume that progress equals the adoption of capitalist, liberal-democratic principles.
- Likewise, modernisation theories assume that development is desirable.

Sociology of Crime and Deviance

1 As Giddens points out, it is impossible to separate hereditary from environmental factors. The aim of most sociologists is to try to understand and explain why people are engaged in deviant activity. For O'Donnell this is, perhaps, less dangerous than regarding them as 'mental' or just downright bad. What solutions to crime do these explanations lead to? Pre-emptive custodial sentencing on the basis of your medical records?

Corrective brain surgery? Or drug treatment programmes similar to the 'aversion therapy' in Anthony Burgess' *A Clockwork Orange*, which denies the anti-hero the right to choose between good and bad? Likewise, Cohen is highly critical of models that presuppose crime can be 'treated'. They fail to acknowledge that criminality may have a social rather than an individual nature.

2 The Marxist and interactionist accounts often draw very similar conclusions. For example, both Lemert's work and Marxism look at the reaction of the police to deviant acts. Likewise, Circourel's work shows that there is ethnic and class bias in how certain groups are treated. Similarly, interactionism implies that no person is inherently criminal nor is any act; it is a social construction. Marxists, for example Hirst and Pearce, argue that it is a construction specific to the capitalist state. A multitude of laws underpin the virtues of hard work, owning property and acquiring possessions by protecting them, whereas the violators are duly punished (whatever their circumstances). However, many Marxists criticise interactionism for failing to fully acknowledge the power-base in society. This is the cause of crime, whereas the interactionist account completely disregards the criminal act and concentrates on the reaction to it instead. The premise for Marxist thought is that Marxists want to change social structures.

Giddens takes issue with this, arguing that the strength of interactionist theory is its ability to demonstrate how the officials of law and order are able to impose definitions of conventional morality, which is an expression of the power and structure of society.

Neo-Marxist approaches have begun to converge with interactionism. Marxist theorists such as Taylor, Walton and Young have adopted a holistic approach to understanding crime in society.

3 According to feminist accounts, women do not commit as much crime because they are controlled better than men. Brownmiller cites the fear of rape/sexual attack in the public sphere by men, which confines their movements. In other words, opportunities are limited. When they are not (re: 'lost letters'), we find the figures are more proportionate.

Carlen describes increasing female criminality as a reaction to unfulfilled 'gender deals', whereas others have looked at the 'emancipation' of women criminals by the women's liberation movement. However, as Box and Hale and Carlen (1985) point out, women's liberation does not adequately explain the increase in women's crime. The most likely offenders, lower class women, were less likely to benefit from the 'liberating' force of feminism.

This contrasts with the biological reasons proposed by Lombrosso and Pollak who believe that female crime is not committed by 'real' women, but either monsters (Myra Hindley), or men (in disguise).

4 Durkheim's work has been highly influential in a number of studies. First, his evaluation of how deviance works in society has been accepted by many, i.e. deviance is universal and normal, it is relative and functional to society. Second, his preoccupation with social bonding has also allowed for a social rather than individual understanding as to why crime and deviance happen. The term anomie, in particular, has been used as a basis in a number of studies.

Merton used this to devise his own sub-cultural theories to explain the prevalence of crime and deviance in contemporary society. Similarly, Cloward and Ohlin (1960), the Chicago School, particularly through the work of Sutherland, Cohen (1955) and Miller (1962) have all used Durkheim's work as a basis, even though they may have arrived at completely different conclusions.

Exam Practice Answers

 1 (a) Conservatism, inspired by the work of Edmund Burke, begins with a negative view of human nature, hence its preoccupation with law and order. It also emphasises evolution, strong nation, traditions and social hierarchies. It has always been a friend to business and the middle class.

Margaret Thatcher's brand of Conservatism drew together two distinct but nevertheless compatible ideologies. Thatcherism bore all the hallmarks of the traditional Conservatism and economic liberalism, which emphasises market forces rather than state interference.

Today's Labour Party, despite its metamorphosis, still bears the hallmarks of socialism. In contrast to the Conservative Party, it assumes that people are essentially good. Socialism emphasises cooperation rather than competition. Socialist-democratic parties favour a mixed economy (i.e. state interference) rather than communism. Principles of welfare have been socialist inspired. The Labour Party has traditionally been seen as the party that redistributes the wealth of the rich to the poor through increased taxation to fund national welfare policies. Its traditional alliance with the trades union movement has made it a natural ally of the working class. Of course, after 18 years in opposition, the transition from 'old' to 'new' Labour to entice the middle class has changed the ideological direction of the party somewhat.

(b) Answers scoring high marks will demonstrate a good awareness of the political system in Britain. The first-past-the-post system has many anomalies, for example the proportion of votes cast is not converted into seats. In recognising this, political parties have focused on targeting those people who can make the difference in marginal seats (constituencies that do not enjoy large majorities by either parties). These people are known as floating voters – they are people with no fixed party loyalty. Political parties have identified 'ideal' voter profiles and they will make a concerted attempt to reach these people either directly or through advertising campaigns.

Exam Practice Answers

A large body of research has concluded that people are more likely to shop around and vote for whoever promises the 'best' deal. This is known as 'pocket-book voting'. Sociologists are interested in how the old certainties of class and voting have disappeared. Answers should demonstrate knowledge of this shift from party identification to consumerist models of voting behaviour.

2

(a) Dependency

(b) Answers should include:

- A description and evaluation of Rostow's theory of modernisation, that countries must work through five stages.
- These stages are technologically-based and have a liberal-democratic, capitalist basis to them.
- Students should also consider Kerr's, Parsons' and McClelland's argument, that underdeveloped countries must adopt a Western world view.
- For Marxists, countries will inevitably move from a position of exploitation to one of true emancipation, a working class for itself.
- This theory is criticised for being too ethnocentric and ignorant of the diversity and richness of different cultures.

(c) Answers should include:

- The historical, political and economic factors that have created an environment where multinational companies enjoy ascendancy. For example, the activities of colonial nations and the power-bloc politics after the Second World War.
- Political and economic trends: the drive towards capitalism, the influence of commercial banks and international aid agencies, such as the IMF.
- The concentration of markets by a few large companies (as Marx envisaged), some richer than the countries they operate within.
- Frank's description of how these powerful companies strike deals with the ruling classes in poorer (satellite) states, which exploits the poor and hinders 'proper' development.

- Jenkins' conclusion that the impact of transnational companies is always negative and leads to undemocratic government and environmental problems (re: 'McLibel' courtcase).
- Some sociologists, for example Harris, recognise that multinational companies bring in new jobs and skills and force technological change.

3

(a) New Right or individualistic approaches.

(b) Murray and Saunders.

(c) Answers should describe and account for:

- The underclass as a distinct group of people who form a layer beneath the working class.
- The universality of descriptions for the underclass. They are multiply-deprived, economically and 'culturally', they live in poor living conditions and so on. They live on the fringes of society.
- Some right-wing critics suggest that deviant behaviour is genetic.
- Dahrendorf treats the existence of an underclass as a result of changing economic circumstances and less demand for unskilled work.
- Marx described the 'lumpenproletariat', as a 'dangerous class' to the working class. They act as a reserve army of labour (whose labour is likely to be cheaper). Workers are less likely to form a radical class conscience if they feel undermined by a group who are willing to work for less.

(d) This question proposes that the working class has either been assimilated into the middle class or it has shrunk due to economic factors, so whilst society as a whole appears to be getting richer, it is leaving a group of people behind. This answer should consider:

- Whether the working class has enjoyed 'movement' to the higher echelons of society.
- Or has the middle class grown? If this is so, it raises questions about social mobility as a whole (re: Glass, Blau and Duncan).
- Limited employment opportunities or the

incentive to work may be curtailed by entering what is known as the 'poverty trap' (by working you are no better off than if you were on benefits). People who remain on benefits tend to get poorer.

It raises the question: what should governments do with the underclass? Should they invest more money into the infrastructure and provide more opportunities for people to improve their skills and life-chances? Or do we leave them to experience market forces, so that rather than being welfare-dependent, they experience and learn that there are consequences for their actions?

4 (a) Statistics on crime are very unreliable. Answers should acknowledge this by looking at the following:

- Official statistics only record crimes recorded by the police. Therefore, sociologists cannot agree on how accurate they are. Some, such as Reiner, argue that as society gathers more material possessions and wealth there is more to steal, hence the relative rise in crime.

- Victimisation studies, such as the British Crime Survey and self-report studies, suggest that the level of crime is much higher than the authorities are aware of.

- Many people do not report crimes, whereas many crimes, for example white-collar crime, are difficult to detect (re: Pearce and Levy).

- On the other hand, the prevalence of household insurance makes people more likely to report property theft/damage. Increasing litigation (personal injuries) may also spark an increase in crime.

- There is also a greater awareness of certain crimes; for example, child abuse seems to be more prevalent today.

- There are inconsistencies in policing and data recording, which affect statistics on crime.

(b) Functionalism is a structural account. Answers should begin with an overview.

- It is concerned with how society should work

for effective social life. Institutions are very important in teaching and reasserting norms and values. For example, the family and education are pervasive and persuasive social institutions.

- Consider Durkheim's definitions of deviance: its universality, normality and relativity.

- Discuss the notion of 'boundary maintaining' or 'bonding' in the face of growing individualism, and the lack of bonding which is divisive. The state of anomie, a feeling of disorientation and not belonging, illuminates the social dynamic of crime and deviant acts (re: *Suicide*).

- Durkheim's work has influenced sub-cultural theorists, who seek to explain the prevalence of crime and deviance in contemporary society. In particular, Merton's (1957) work is an extension of Durkheim's work.

- Other theorists and studies, connected to but not necessarily defined as functionalist, such as Cloward and Ohlin (1960) and Edwin H. Sutherland, have presented a better understanding of how and why sub-cultural groups exist.

(c) Your answer should focus on the following:

- a description and evaluation of physiological and psychological accounts

- a review of the social construction of crime (re: Foucault)

It should incorporate an appraisal of:

- structural accounts – functionalism versus Marxism

- the interactionist approach, especially, Becker, Lemert and Circourel, who offer another account of how 'social situation' determines deviance

- how, for feminists, sex or gender is highly significant but equally problematic in patriarchal society

- Hall's and Gilroy's work, which places emphasis on ethnicity.